LEISUREGUIDE

AA

The
Cotswolds

AA Publishing

Author: Christopher Knowles

Page layout: Jo Tapper

Produced by AA Publishing
© Automobile Association
Developments Ltd 1996, 1999,
2002.

Published by AA Publishing (a
trading name of Automobile
Association Developments Limited,
whose registered office is
Millstream, Maidenhead Road,
Windsor, Berkshire, SL4 5GD.
Registered Number 1878835)

First edition published 1996,
reprinted 1996, 1997, 1998.
Second edition 1999,
reprinted 2000 (twice).
Third edition 2002.

Ordnance Survey® This product
includes
mapping data licensed from
Ordnance Survey® with the
permission of the Controller of Her
Majesty's Stationery Office.
© Crown copyright 2002. All rights
reserved. Licence number 399221

Mapping produced by the
Cartographic Department of The
Automobile Association. A00691.

ISBN 07495 3292 0

A CIP catalogue record for this
book is available from the British
Library.

Gazetteer map references are taken
from the National Grid and can be
used in conjunction with Ordnance
Survey maps and atlases. Places
featured in this guide will not
necessarily be found on the maps
at the back of the book.

All the walks are on rights of way,
permissive paths or on routes
where de facto access for walkers is
accepted. On routes which are not
on legal rights of way, but where
access for walkers is allowed by
local agreements, no implication of
a right of way is intended.

The contents of this book are
believed correct at the time of
printing. Nevertheless, the
publishers cannot accept
responsibility for errors or
omissions, or for changes in
details given in this guide or for the
consequences of any reliance on
the information it provides. We
have tried to ensure accuracy in
this book, but things do change
and we would be grateful if readers
would advise us of any inaccuracies
they may encounter.

Visit the AA Publishing website at
www.theAA.com

Colour reproduction by L C Repro

Printed and bound by G. Canale &
C. s.p.a., Torino, Italy

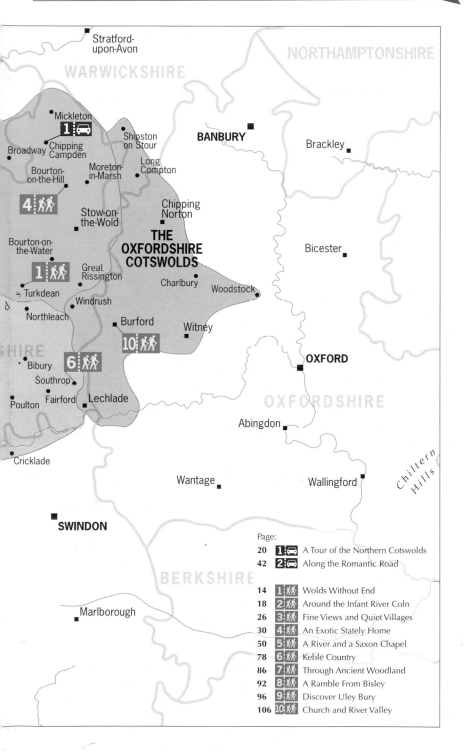

Stratford-upon-Avon

NORTHAMPTONSHIRE

WARWICKSHIRE

Mickleton

1 🚗

Shipston on Stour

BANBURY

Brackley

Broadway

Chipping Campden

Bourton-on-the-Hill

Moreton-in-Marsh

Long Compton

4 🚶🚶

Stow-on-the-Wold

Chipping Norton

THE OXFORDSHIRE COTSWOLDS

Bicester

Bourton-on-the-Water

1 🚶🚶

Great Rissington

Charlbury

Woodstock

Turkdean

Windrush

Northleach

Burford

Witney

OXFORD

10 🚶🚶

Bibury

6 🚶🚶

Southrop

Poulton Fairford Lechlade

OXFORDSHIRE

Abingdon

Cricklade

Wantage

Wallingford

Chiltern Hills

SWINDON

BERKSHIRE

Marlborough

Introducing The Cotswolds

RELAX...
Tranquil moments are
not hard to find in
the depths of the
Cotswolds

WAYS TO GO...
The Cotswold Way links some of the best villages
between Bath and Chipping Campden

A FLAVOUR OF THE COTSWOLDS

If anywhere satisfies that image of England, where unspoilt villages with medieval church tower, ancient pub and clear streams sit in idyllic rural tranquillity, then it is the Cotswolds.

The wolds are an area of undulations which roll away eastwards from a limestone escarpment between Bath and Chipping Campden. On the plateau and among its folds villages built entirely out of gilded limestone and stone slate have changed only little from when sheep covered the land lying between them; for it was the medieval wool trade, and later the cloth weaving industry, that made the Cotswolds famous.

Although the Cotswolds are now invariably associated with the picturesque, the area is much more than that. History has produced magnificent wool churches, manor houses and Roman villas; art has brought the music of Vaughan Williams and the literature of Laurie Lee. Nature provides remarkable views of the vale and the River Severn. In short, there is something for everyone.

COTSWOLD SILK
Textiles have long been a base of wealth in the area, and craftspeople may still be found, plying skills old and new

COTSWOLD WILDLIFE
Wildlife flourishes in meadows, on ancient grassland, and in the protected area of the Cotswold Water Park

COTSWOLD PLANTS
Woodland flowers abound, including springtime carpets of bluebells, primroses and ramsons (wild garlic)

WILLIAM MORRIS
William Morris, the great champion of the 19th-century Arts and Crafts Movement which promoted the tradition of fine craftsmanship, made his home at Kelmscot, near Faringdon

MAKE A FRIEND...
The Cotswold Farm Park at Guiting Power preserves our ancient breeds and offers a great day out

CHEESE ROLLING
As sports go, the rolling of Double Gloucester cheeses down a 45° hill is strictly local to Coopers Hill!

STANWAY GATEHOUSE
Stanway is a superb example of a cohesive village clustered around its fine Jacobean manor house

ODDA'S CHAPEL
Spanning the ages, Odda's Chapel at Deerhurst, dating back to 1056, was rediscovered in the late 19th century

LAURIE LEE
In **Cider With Rosie** (1959), writer and poet Laurie Lee evoked a rich, timeless portrait of his Cotswold childhood

LAURIE LEE
Cider with Rosie

CHIPPING CAMPDEN CHURCH
The church at Chipping Campden is a fine example of Perpendicular architecture

TEN BEST VILLAGES

Chipping Campden
Blockley
Wootton-under-Edge
Winchcombe
Painswick
Burford
Stow-on-the-Wold
Minster Lovell
Charlbury
Sapperton

THE ESSENTIAL COTSWOLDS

If you have little time and you want to sample the essence of the Cotswolds:

See the views from the Cotswold edge, particularly from Leckhampton or Cleeve Hills or Uley Bury... **Walk** a section of the Cotswold Way or along the Coln Valley... **Visit** Stanway House with its charming gatehouse... **Climb** Sandhurst Hill by the River Severn and look back across the vale to the Cotswold escarpment... **Treat** yourself to afternoon tea at the Pump Rooms in Bath or a beer from the local Donnington brewery at the Mount Inn, Stanton... **Experience** a day at the races at the Cheltenham Gold Cup... **Discover** the 'lost' Saxon chapel built by Earl Odda... **Marvel** at the greatest collection of waterfowl in the world at Slimbridge... **Visit** Blenheim, one of Britain's grandest palaces, a gift from Queen Anne to the victorious Duke of Marlborough... **Admire** the church at Chipping Campden, perhaps the finest of the many magnificent wool churches.

A Weekend in the Cotswolds, Day One

For many people a weekend break or a long weekend is a popular way of spending their leisure time.

These four pages offer a loosely planned itinerary designed to ensure that you make the most of your time and see and enjoy the very best the area has to offer.

Options for wet weather are given and places with gazetteer entries are in **bold**.

Friday Night

Stay at the Painswick Hotel in the village of Painswick, a hotel full of character, serving fine food in elegant surroundings. Alternatively, in Cheltenham, the Wyastone, Milton House and George all offer good value in a more central location. In the evening wander around Cheltenham the 'Centre for the Cotswolds', a town of considerable charm and elegance, of handsome, wide streets lined with Regency style villas and terraces.

Look out for the surprising architectural details, left, in Cheltenham's Montpellier Street

Enjoy the magnificent gardens at Snowshill, below

Saturday Morning

If it's raining return to **Cheltenham** and keep under cover in the Art Gallery and Museum and the Pittville Pump Room which has an imaginative costume exhibition; after lunch go to **Snowshill**.

Head up the escarpment on to the wolds through Prestbury and over **Cleeve Hill**. Stop near **Belas Knap**, one of the best-preserved Neolithic barrows in the country, to enjoy the view across to **Winchcombe**. Then

Don't miss the fine Norman doorway on the church at Guiting Power, right

visit the town, its handsome church and **Sudeley Castle and Gardens**, one of England's most delightful historic houses with many royal connections; the entrance is down Vineyard Street.

After Sudeley take the byways east and north and don't miss **Guiting Power**, **Naunton** and **Snowshill**.

Detour from Winchcombe for a glimpse of beautiful Hailes Abbey, below

Saturday Lunch

For lunch The Plaisterers Arms in **Winchcombe** is a lively pub with good food and a large garden. Alternatively, there are good village pubs in both **Guiting Power** and **Naunton**.

Enjoy the scenic delights of Chipping Campden, right

Saturday Afternoon

Continue via **Snowshill** (only visit **Snowshill Manor** if you can get in as it opens, before the crowds) to **Chipping Campden** and devote at least a couple of hours to exploring this wonderful village. Drive to **Burford** via **Moreton-in-Marsh** and **Stow-on-the-Wold**.

Allow time off from shopping in Burford to explore the old church, below

Saturday Night

The Bay Tree in **Burford**, dating back to Tudor times, is luxurious with four-poster beds that have never left the building. The Lamb is a cheaper and excellent alternative.

A Weekend in The Cotswolds, Day Two

Your second and final day starts with a pleasant walk to two of the charming villages in the Windrush Valley, before driving west to the medieval wool town of Cirencester, which is easily explored on foot. Round off your weekend in the Cotswolds with a visit to the Roman city of Bath.

Sunday Morning

If it is raining go straight to **Bath** with its many attractions, No 1 Royal Crescent, the Roman Baths and Pump Room and the Building of Bath Museum to name only a few.

If the weather is fine take a stroll east along the **River Windrush** to visit **Widford** or even **Swinbrook**. Then drive to **Cirencester** via the A361 and the A417 through **Fairford** (with the spectacular stained glass in the church) or via the A40 and the B4425 through **Bibury** (picturesque but frequently crowded).

Cirencester, the most important of the Cotswold wool towns in the Middle Ages is most easily explored on foot and the Market Square is the most convenient place to begin discovery of the town.

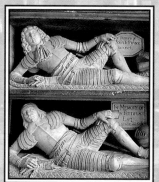

If the weather is fine, explore the Cotswold villages at leisure, above

See the Fettiplace memorial in Swinbrooke Church, left

Stop off in Fairford to admire the church glass, below

Enjoy lunchtime hospitality in Cirencester, right

Stroll around the delights of Bath, below

Take in the more austere elegance of Tetbury's fine church, bottom

Sunday Lunch

The Swan at Swinbrook serves good lunches, whilst near Bibury, on the Fosse Way, the ancient Fossebridge Inn has a spacious garden by a stream. In **Cirencester** itself there are inns on the Market Square near the church.

Sunday Afternoon

If time permits a late afternoon visit to **Bath** can be recommended, as the tourists are beginning to disperse. One of the most magnificent towns in Europe, Bath is known chiefly for its Roman baths and for the elegance of its Georgian architecture.

To see another side of the Cotswolds, drive along the Golden Valley towards **Stroud** and then head south through **Nailsworth** to **Tetbury**, with its charming Georgian church and magnificent Market House.

The Northern Cotswolds

In this book the line between the northern and southern Cotswolds runs between Painswick and Northleach.

Generally speaking the north is considered more picturesque. Its villages, Bourton-on-the-Water, the Slaughters, Stanton and so on, are carved out of the local building stone, here the colour of biscuit and liquid gold. Many have barely changed since the time when the wool industry became the cloth industry and moved to the steeper southern valleys. The countryside of this northern area rolls, undulating wolds open to the sky, scooped here and there with wide valleys run through with shallow streams.

Handsome cottages line Blockley's High Street, with purple aubretia spilling out on to the pavement

THE FOSSE WAY

Blockley lies to the west of the Fosse Way, the Roman road which runs diagonally across the Cotswolds, through Moreton-in-Marsh, Stow-on-the-Wold and Cirencester, linking Exeter with Lincoln, a distance of 182 miles (291.2km). It is said that its route never varies more than 6 miles (9.6km) from true.

BLOCKLEY Gloucestershire Map ref SP1634

A handsome village lacking the obvious charm of many of its neighbours but with a subtle appeal undoubtedly worthy of attention, Blockley was a silk town and by 1880, just before the failure of the industry in the area, there were six mills here employing some 500 people supplying Coventry's ribbon manufacturers. Many of the weavers' cottages remain, the older ones towards the village centre, the 19th-century silk workers' cottages terraced along the northern edge. One of the old mills can be seen beyond a pool near the church, whilst the village is dotted with houses of varying ages and appeal.

The church, with its Norman chancel, is unusually

large, testament to its early status, with a tower that was completed only in 1725. Within is a Jacobean pulpit and some interesting brasses. There are plenty of good walks to be taken around Blockley, which is blessed with two pubs, one of which is also a hotel.

BOURTON-ON-THE-WATER Gloucestershire
Map ref SP1620

The busiest honeypot in the area is this attractive village, watered by the River Windrush which flows proudly along the main street beneath a succession of graceful footbridges, earning for Bourton the soubriquet 'the Venice of the Cotswolds'. A tourist mecca, and frankly to be avoided if rural calm is what you yearn for, the village does have a lot to offer in the way of attractions – Birdland is an authentic zoo for birds, with a remarkable collection of penguins, some of which have come from the owner's islands in the South Atlantic. There is also a Model Village (Bourton in miniature), a motor museum, a perfume factory and a model railway exhibition, all within walking distance of each other and of the main street. Just off the main street is Bourton's church, a mixture of elements, with a medieval chancel, Victorian nave and distinctive Georgian tower, complete with skull on the exterior, a salutary reminder of our mortality.

Bourton can be best appreciated in the evenings after the crowds have dispersed, when a walk around its back streets and along the river is a very pleasant experience.

Just to the east of Bourton are a series of gravel pits that, now filled with water, have become sanctuaries for waterfowl and make a very pleasant walk by following the path across Station Road from the car park.

West of Bourton is a group of villages, Notgrove, Cold Aston, Turkdean and Hazleton, that are featured in both the Walk on page 14 and the Car Tour on page 20. Folly Farm Waterfowl, near Notgrove, is an interesting collection of rare waterfowl, wildfowl and poultry.

BIRDLAND

Birdland was established by Len Hill, who purchased two small islands in the South Atlantic some years ago. These islands, part of the Falkland Islands group, are inhabited by penguins and a considerable variety of other birds, some of which can be seen along with macaws, parrots and cockatoos, in interesting and varied habitats on the banks of the River Windrush at Bourton. The antics of a large colony of penguins can be viewed through a glass-sided pool.

Elegant footbridges spanning the Windrush distinguish Bourton-on-the-Water's main thoroughfare

Wolds Without End

A long circular walk to introduce you to the real 'wolds', of undulating land and barely visited villages.

Time: 4 hours. Distance: 8 miles (12.9km)
Location: 2½ miles (4km) northwest of Northleach.
Start: From Northleach travel northwest on the A40, after 2 miles (3.2km) turn left on to the Salt Way and park in the lay-by on the left. Walk to the junction with A40, cross the road and turn left to the Puesdown Inn
(OS grid ref: SP085171.)
OS Map: Outdoor Leisure 45 (The Cotswolds) 1:25,000.
See Key to Walks on page 121.

Just before the green, alongside some farm buildings, turn right down a track to a gate. Go through the gate, cross a yard to another gate to enter a field and follow a track which heads towards Hazleton. After 800 yards (732m), at a shallow valley, the path divides.

Bear left through a gate, continue in the direction of a fir plantation and head up towards the village of Hazleton. The track becomes a lane; pass a few cottages and then turn left to retrace your steps to the starting point .

ROUTE DIRECTIONS

Facing the Puesdown Inn go into the yard and walk to the left of the pub. Cross a stile and keep to the margin of the field, with the wall on the left, until you meet a farm track. Turn left and continue to the village of **Hazleton**. Turn right on a lane into Hazleton and then shortly turn left at a junction. Follow this road as it curves to the right and then shortly turn left again at the next junction.

Head in the direction of the church and at a crossroads go straight ahead on to a good farm track. Continue towards the farm, which you pass on your right, and then alongside a wood. Where the wood ends carry straight on to pass through two fields with a stone wall on your left. Pass through a gate, with a wall to the left, and continue by fields to another avenue of trees. Go through here to a road, with **Salperton Park** and church visible through the trees before you.

Turn right along the road for about three quarters of a mile (1.2km) until you reach the modern barn by Farhill Farm. Immediately after, just before the older house and barn of Farhill Farm, leave the road, bear to the right of the farm buildings and keep to a rough track which descends, by a tumbledown stone wall, to a large concave field. Bear, briefly, slightly right and then turn left to descend directly along the bed of the field, between its shallow slopes, to the bottom, where you will find a gateway. Go through into another small valley at the bottom of rough meadow and turn right. Keep to the left of a dying tree on a ledge to find a gateway in a fence. Go through the gate and turn left. Climb a grassy track towards a farm building, passing through two gates.

The second gate brings you on to a firm farm track by the farm building, Kitehill Barn. Pass to the right of the barn and continue to the top of a rise which will bring you to a road at the gates of Notgrove Manor.

To visit **Notgrove** (off the map) turn left here and then after 200 yards (183m) turn right along a lane towards the village. To continue on the main route, turn right and proceed towards **Turkdean**.

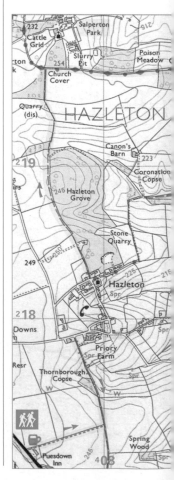

POINTS OF INTEREST

Hazleton
A quiet village on the old Salt Way with a church that has a handsome Norman south doorway and a large stone font.

Salperton
Salperton is really Salperton Park, a handsome 17th-century manor house that was greatly altered in the 19th century. Next to the manor is the church with a Norman chancel arch and a medieval wall painting of a skeleton holding a scythe and an arrow, a reminder,

presumably, of Man's frail mortality. There are also several memorials to the occupants of Salperton House. This lonely village is still attached to the manor and the whole estate once came up for sale for £10 million.

Notgrove
A lovely wold village whose church, though largely Norman, has a primitive Saxon crucifix on the exterior of the east wall. Inside are monuments to the Whittington family; the most famous was Sir Richard,

or 'Dick' Whittington, who became Lord Mayor of London. Northwest of the village is Notgrove Long Barrow, a Neolithic long cairn, which was excavated in the 1880s and again in 1931. It consists of two pairs of side chambers and another at the end of a gallery; several skeletons were also discovered here.

Turkdean
This strangely named hamlet has an interesting Norman church, which contains a large 15th-century stone pulpit.

BECKFORD SILK

The silk industry is not entirely new to the Cotswolds – towns such as Blockley thrived on it for a brief period in the 18th and 19th centuries. Beckford Silk has produced hand-printed silk since 1975, originally in the converted coach house of the Old Vicarage, and now at its present workshop at the edge of the village. Silk is imported from China, whilst the dyes used in the process are from Switzerland. The silk is printed by means of screens which match the desired pattern and are made up in such a way that only one colour dye is released at a time through the screen on to the material.

BREDON HILL Worcestershire

Map ref SO9640

The landscape north of Tewkesbury, just within the borders of Worcestershire, is dominated by the bulk of Bredon Hill, 960-feet (295m) high, a huge Cotswold outlier (outcrop of rocks) shaped like an upturned saucer. The countryside of the area is, however, substantially different from the Cotswolds proper – building in stone is much less in evidence, the landscape more in tune with the surrounding Vale of Evesham. The hill itself is an excellent place for rambling and indeed for brambling, because in the autumn the lanes and tracks that criss-cross Bredon's slopes are rich in blackberries.

At its summit is Parson's Folly, an 18th-century tower standing amid the remains of an Iron-Age hillfort where a number of bodies were discovered where they had fallen during some ancient battle, probably against the invading Belgae some 2,000 years ago.

Below and roundabout are several villages of interest. At Beckford silk continues to be printed by hand, whilst at Kemerton the footpath takes you through the exotic gardens of the old priory. Overbury, with its variety of half-timbered and stone houses, is often thought of as one of the loveliest villages in Worcestershire. Bredon itself, immortalised in John Moore's affectionate story of mid-20th century rural life, *Brensham Village*, is noted for its magnificent 14th-century tithe barn, which is now in the care of the National Trust.

Don't miss the tithe barn in Bredon village, which was built to house the tax in kind levied by the Church

BROADWAY Worcestershire
Map ref SP0937

Broadway is almost synonymous with the Cotswolds and yet, with its wide main street (built to cover two streams that run either side of the older road) ploughing busily up the lower slopes of the escarpment, it is hardly a typical Cotswold village. Most of the houses that line the street in glorious array date from the 16th, 17th and 18th centuries. Some were inns, for Broadway was an important staging post on the London and Worcester route, following the construction of the road up Fish Hill in the early 18th century; the Lygon Arms, now one of the most famous hotels in the country, is a reminder of that period. Later the village was the object of the attentions of William Morris, and a number of other luminaries from the arts, including Henry James.

Everything in the village (except Broadway Tower and perhaps the old church) can be discovered on foot and the completion of the bypass makes Broadway a pleasant place for wandering. Broadway's original church, St Eadburgha's, some way out, on the Snowshill Road, is worth a visit to elude the crowds.

The town is overlooked by Broadway Tower, a glowering piece of Gothic folly on one of the highest points of the Cotswolds. It is a steep walk from the village, set on the edge of the escarpment in a country park. There are exhibitions, and an observation room with a telescope, giving wonderful views. The nearby village of Buckland, which is within walking distance of Broadway, is a pretty village with a particularly fine 15th-century parsonage. The church contains some Jacobean seating and a finely worked panel said to have come from Hailes Abbey, near Winchcombe.

Old St Eadburgha's became redundant when the Victorians built a new parish church in Broadway

BROADWAY TOWER

The 65-foot (20m) tower was designed by James Wyatt for the 6th Earl of Coventry and was built in 1799 using Portland stone, more suitably portentous than the local stone. William Morris stayed here with the Pre-Raphaelites Burne-Jones and Rossetti and there is an interesting exhibition within. Try to go on a clear day when you can enjoy the finest of views from its crenellated roof.

Around the Infant River Coln

A fairly short and undemanding walk that offers an excellent Cotswold panorama and explores two of the lesser-known villages in the area. Delightful in the summer months, yet equally enjoyable in winter, since the paths are mostly resistant to mud.

Time: 2½ hours. Distance: 5 miles (8km).
Location: 6 miles (9.7km) east of Cheltenham.
Start: Syreford Farm, just outside Syreford. A quarter of a mile (0.4km) north of the A436. Park carefully and with consideration on the verge opposite the farm.
(OS grid ref: SP030202.)
OS Map: Outdoor Leisure 45 (The Cotswolds) 1:25,000.
See Key to Walks on page 121.

ROUTE DIRECTIONS

Take the track opposite Syreford Farm. Climb uphill passing a tin-roofed barn, and continue ascending between fields as the track curves left and right, with good views opening up behind you across a gently rolling Cotswold landscape. Below, away to your left in the distance, are **Sevenhampton** and **Brockhampton** lying in the infant Coln Valley.

Pass through the trees of Elsdown Covert and emerge out on to the crest of the hill beyond a gateway. Descend to a house and cross a road on to a metalled lane, signposted 'Guiting Power and Winchcombe'. Shortly, descend sharply beside Baker's Wood and turn left along the narrow lane, arrowed Brockhampton.

Follow the gently undulating lane for three-quarters of a mile (1.2km), with views of Cleeve Hill, and bear sharp left into the village. Bear right by the telephone box, then head left by the sign for the pub, and soon pass the Craven Arms. Take the grassy path ahead, waymarked 'Sevenhampton, via St Andrew's Church', pass the infant River Coln, then bear right and enter a field. Bear left and follow the trail over a shallow rise towards Manor Farm.

Keep to the left of the farm, pass through a gate, then proceed along the right-hand stone wall of a meadow and enter a graveyard. Bear right, then left and pass St Andrew's Church to reach a gate and a lane. Cross over, go through a kissing gate into a meadow, then keep right of the tree in front of you, and descend to another gate and join a defined path. Descend past a house, cross a stile fording a stream, then, at a fork of paths, keep right along the

Creeper adorns the mellow walls of Brockhampton Manor

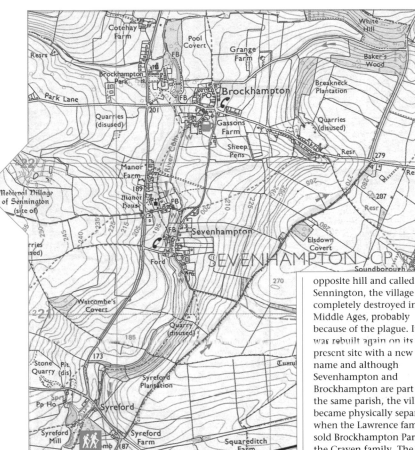

lower trail to a road, also forded by the stream. Turn left, then in a few yards, turn right passing a row of houses.

Proceed through two gates into a field, then turn immediately right and head for a metal gate, keeping the barn on your left. Head towards woodland, pass through two further gates and join a clear woodland path to emerge by a house. Follow a farm track to the road at **Syreford**, turn left, pass the Gallery, then after 200 yards (182m) arrive back at Syreford Farm.

POINTS OF INTEREST

Brockhampton

An attractive village with a handsome mainly 19th-century manor house, Brockhampton Park, once known for its deer park and herd of white deer. The local pub, the Craven Arms, is named after the family who lived at the manor for many years. The pub is adjoined by the remains, notably the distinctive red-brick chimney, of the older brewery.

Sevenhampton

Originally located on the opposite hill and called Sennington, the village was completely destroyed in the Middle Ages, probably because of the plague. It was rebuilt again on its present site with a new name and although Sevenhampton and Brockhampton are part of the same parish, the villages became physically separate when the Lawrence family sold Brockhampton Park to the Craven family. The church is originally Norman, though added to and improved in the 15th century by John Camber, a wealthy wool merchant. It is very pretty, with an attractive wooden ceiling and miniature flying buttresses.

Syreford

A small, quiet hamlet with a very pretty mill house on the banks of the River Coln. Among the items discovered during the excavations of the Roman settlement here, was a very handsome statuette, just four inches high, of Mars, the god of war.

A Tour of the Northern Cotswolds

Starting from Chipping Campden, the finest of the Cotswold wool towns, with a magnificent church and every house a gem, this circular drive of 75 miles (120.7km) takes in many of the highlights of the northern Cotswolds as well as several worthy, though less visited, places in the area.

ROUTE DIRECTIONS

See Key to Car Tours on page 120.

From the Market Hall on Chipping Campden's High Street head for Mickleton on the B4081, turning right just after the end of the speed restrictions. Soon turn right again for Hidcote Boyce. Continue to a crossroads and turn left for Hidcote Bartrim, Mickleton and Hidcote Gardens. Keep following signs for **Hidcote Gardens** and **Kiftsgate Court Gardens** (both open to the public). Drive past Kiftsgate, signed 'Quinton' and 'Stratford', until you reach a junction at a corner. Turn right and continue to Ilmington. Just after

entering Ilmington turn right for Chipping Campden, then left for Shipston, keeping left at the war memorial. Pass the Red Lion pub, continuing in the direction of Stratford. At the end of the village turn right and drive to Armscote, where you pass the Waggon Wheel Inn, and turn right for Blackwell and Tredington. Soon, just after a thatched barn and a pond, turn left for Tredington.

Continue to the A429 and turn left towards Warwick. At a roundabout turn right to join the A3400, signed 'Tredington, Shipston,

Charlton Abbots clusters amid the trees

Oxford'. About a mile (1.6km) beyond Tredington turn left for Honington, through pineapple-topped gates. Drive through Honington then turn right at a junction for Barcheston and after a further half mile (0.8km) go left at a T-junction opposite farm buildings for St Dennis and Tysoe. Pass a crossroads for St Dennis Farm and continue for about 2 miles (3.2km) to another crossroads; go forward, signed 'Tysoe', and continue, to join another road at a corner. Turn right here and then fairly soon go left towards **Compton Wynyates** house and Epwell. Follow the Epwell signs. Turn right at a crossroads, and continue in the direction of Banbury and Sibfords (although you may wish to follow signs to Epwell where there is a pub).

On the main route continue to the B4035 and turn right, soon arriving at Lower Brailes. Drive past the George Hotel and turn left, just after a school sign, into Sutton Lane for Stourton, Cherington and Long Compton. Halfway through Sutton-under-Brailes turn left for Stourton, Cherington and Long Compton. Drive through Stourton, then Cherington and continue to follow signs for Long Compton until meeting the A3400. Turn left and drive through Long Compton. Ignore the first sign for Little Rollright almost at the end of the village, but take the second, after about a mile (1.6km) on the right, for Little Rollright, to see the **Rollright Stones**, prehistoric standing stones of uncertain origin, and Little Compton. Continue to the A44, turn right and then immediately left on to the A436.

Continue following signs for Stow, then turn left, signed

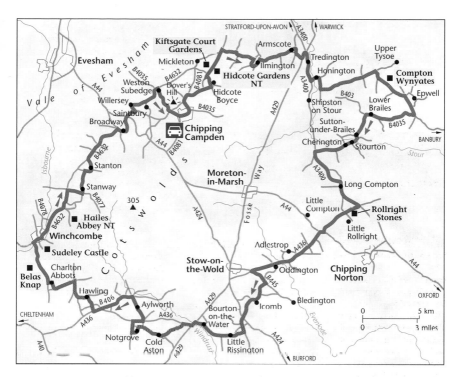

'Bledington'. Keep going to cross a bridge, then immediately turn right for Icomb. Turn right at Icomb war memorial and then left at a T-junction towards Little Rissington. Cross the A424 and continue for almost a mile (1.6km) to turn right at crossroads. Drive through Little Rissington and then Bourton-on-the-Water, aiming for the A429, where you turn left. Soon fork right on to the A436 and after half a mile (0.8km) fork left to Cold Aston. Pass through the village and after just over a mile (1.6km) turn left at a junction for Notgrove. Go through the village and turn right at a junction, signed 'Cheltenham'. At the A436 turn right and then shortly left for Aylworth.

Continue through Aylworth to a crossroads, turning left on the B4068 towards

Cheltenham. Join the A436 and then soon turn right following signs to Hawling and Winchcombe. Continue to Hawling, pass the church and then turn right at a T-junction for Roel and Winchcombe. At the crossroads turn left for Charlton Abbots. Continue for about 1½ miles (2.4km), turn right to bypass Charlton Abbots and then at a T-junction turn right for Winchcombe. Keep going towards Winchcombe, passing the Neolithic barrow **Belas Knap**.

Eventually you come to the B4632 – turn right to go through Winchcombe, continue for 2 miles (3.2km) to a roundabout and turn right on to the B4077, following signs for 'Stow'.

Continue for about a mile (1.6km), then turn left at the war memorial for Stanton. Pass Stanway, then after

about 1½ miles (2.4km) turn right. Drive through Stanton, following 'Broadway' sign, to eventually rejoin the B4632. Turn right here following the B4632 'Stratford' signs. Turn right, then left through Broadway to reach the roundabout on the A44. Take the second exit off the roundabout still following the B4632 'Stratford' signs to Willersey.

Continue through Willersey and come to a roundabout. Turn right here and continue towards Weston Subedge. Go through Weston Subedge and turn right for Dover's Hill. Continue up Dover's Hill, with fine views, to a major crossroads, go forward and down the hill to return to Chipping Campden and the start of the tour.

Chipping Campden is, for many, the epitome of Cotswold charm

THE COTSWOLD OLYMPICKS
Dover's Hill is the site of the Cotswold Olympicks, inaugurated in 1612 by Robert Dover and specialising in sports both conventional and unconventional. The games flourished until 1853 by which time they had begun to resemble an annual bacchanalia.

The modern games, revived at the time of the Festival of Britain in 1951, include an evening procession of competitors followed by an appearance of hounds, various eccentric and boisterous events, and finally a torchlit Scuttlebrook procession down to Chipping Campden. On the following day the traditional Saturday Scuttlebrook Wake takes place in Chipping Campden.

CHIPPING CAMPDEN Gloucestershire Map ref SP1539
The loveliest village in the Cotswolds is a gilded masterpiece. The main street curves in a shallow arc lined with a succession of houses each grafted to the next but each with its own distinctive embellishments. As the name suggests (Chipping means market), Chipping Campden was a market town, certainly one of the most important of the medieval wool towns in the Cotswolds, famous throughout Europe. The legacy of that fame and prosperity is everything that gives the town its character. The town subsequently dozed for centuries until Edward Ashbee moved his Guild of Handicraft here from London in 1902. Although the guild foundered within a few years, it has left its mark so that a few craftsmen continue their work today.

Campden's church, at the north end of the town, is perhaps the finest wool church in the Cotswolds, with a magnificent 120-foot (36m) tower and a spacious, almost austere interior which contains the largest brass, to William Grevel, in the county. The Gainsborough Chapel houses the fine 17th-century marble tomb of Sir Baptist Hicks and his wife who built the nearby stone almshouses in 1612, as well as Campden House, the remains of which can still be seen opposite the almshouses. Campden House was, perhaps deliberately, razed during the Civil War to prevent it falling into Cromwell's hands. Part of it has been restored and can be rented from the Landmark Trust as a holiday home.

Among many fine houses in the village is Grevel House, on the High Street, opposite Church Street. It belonged to William Grevel, the wool merchant largely responsible for the church in its current form and who, it is supposed, was the model for the merchant in Chaucer's *Canterbury Tales*.

Just off Leysbourne, which is the northern extension of the High Street, is the Ernest Wilson Memorial Garden, a charming little botanical enclave snug in the shadow of the church. It commemorates the famous and eccentric plant collector who was born here in 1876. In the middle of the village, on stone pillars, is the 1627 Market Hall, also built by Baptist Hicks 'for the sale of butter, cheese and poultry'.

The village is overlooked by Dover's Hill, from where there are magnificent views across the Vale of Evesham.

THE GUITINGS
Gloucestershire Map ref SP0928/SP0924

The valley running east of Winchcombe, following the course of the River Windrush towards Bourton, is sprinkled with some charming villages. There are two Guitings, for example – the intriguingly named Temple Guiting and Guiting Power. Temple Guiting takes its name from the Knights Templar who owned the manor from the 12th century, and is a pretty village among trees at the edge of the stream. Its church is an interesting mix of styles, and although there are fragmentary remains of the Norman construction, its tower is 18th century, as are the pulpit and the windows, with stained glass of the 16th century.

Guiting Power, a couple of miles to the south of Temple Guiting, is clustered around a small green, and is a perfect example of how the English village can seem to have been carved from the earth it is built on.

The church, to the south of the village, has an exceptionally fine Norman south doorway, although the interior is rather uninspiring. The foundations of a Saxon chapel have been discovered just to the north of the existing church.

Guiting Power hosts a small but significant annual music and arts festival in July.

AN ENCHANTING PASTORAL SCENE
It is a pleasant walk from Guiting Power to Naunton, a prodigiously winsome village. The River Windrush traverses the village close to its centre, where lovingly tended gardens, belonging to cottages and houses of great charm, are scattered about a green near the church. Down by the stream is a huge 17th-century dovecot.

The pleasantly lit interior of the church at Guiting Power

**MAJOR LAWRENCE
JOHNSTON**

When Major Lawrence Johnston, an avid horticulturist, acquired Hidcote Manor in 1905, there was nothing there, apart from the house, some walls, a cedar tree and a number of beeches. He succeeded in bringing about a transformation and created an elaborate garden that is generally considered to be the most influential of the 20th century. It is partly based on the traditional rural cottage garden but also on the tenets of Gertrude Jekyll, an advocate of 'natural gardening', who at the turn of the century was instrumental in incorporating elements of heath and woodland into cottage gardens.

HIDCOTE MANOR GARDEN AND KIFTSGATE COURT GARDEN Gloucestershire Map ref SP1742

Just four miles (6.4km) northeast of Chipping Campden, in the hamlet of Hidcote Bartrim, is the National Trust property of Hidcote Manor, famous above all for its series of scenic gardens which have transformed a 17th-century house of comparative mediocrity into an inspiration for modern gardeners.

The 11-acre garden, an imaginative mix of formal design and seeming haphazard planting, was created over the course of 40 years from 1905 onwards after Hidcote was purchased by Major Lawrence Johnston, the great horticulturist. There are, in fact, a number of separate gardens, each created to a different design, each producing different colours of flowers and shrubs, the effect heightened by the use of walls and hedges of copper and green beech, box, holly, hornbeam and yew, which also protect the plants, many of which are rare or unique, from the severe Cotswold winds. Within the hedges are the formal Bathing Pool Garden, the Fuchsia Garden, the White Garden and the Kitchen Garden as well as a less formal creation by a stream. In addition there are a beech avenue and a lime alley. Visitors can enjoy magnificent views of hill and vale from various points throughout the gardens .

Kiftsgate Court Garden, only a short distance from Hidcote Manor, is situated on a wooded slope from where there are fine views across the Oxfordshire wolds. Although less celebrated than Hidcote, the gardens nonetheless deserve a visit. The house is largely Victorian, whilst the gardens were created after World War I by Heather Muir. The terraced areas above the scarp are a paradise of colourful flower beds and shrubs, whilst the slope is covered in pines. Above all the gardens are famous for a collection of old-fashioned roses, including *Rosa* 'Filipes Kiftsgate', which is believed to be the largest rose in England.

The famous White Garden at Hidcote, remarkable in its day, has inspired many imitators

HILLS AND COMMONS

The northern part of the Cotswold escarpment is higher and is notable for hills offering wonderful views across the Severn Vale to Wales. Best known is Cleeve Hill, at 1,083 foot (333m) the highest point of the Cotswolds and the highest, furthermore, in lowland England. It is a windswept plateau straddling the way between Cheltenham and Winchcombe, distinctive for the cluster of radio towers which are starkly visible from almost everywhere in the area. Part of it is a municipal golf course, but most of it is ancient common, pricked out with gorse bushes on a carpet of coarse grass, and much favoured by horses from nearby stables, as well as birds, orchids and butterflies. It is a pleasant walk across the hill to Winchcombe, via either Belas Knap or Postlip.

Leckhampton Hill overlooks Cheltenham. Like many of the hills the length of the Cotswold escarpment, it was an Iron-Age hillfort built by the Celtic La Tene people who arrived from the continent from 300 BC. More recently, Leckhampton's quarries provided much of the stone for Regency Cheltenham. Just below the lip on the west side of the hill is a famous local landmark, the Devil's Chimney, a pinnacle of stone left behind by 18th-century quarriers, said to arise from Hell.

Just south of Leckhampton is Crickley Hill. In part a country park, it is a good place for family walking, with a number of trails of varying lengths. Here, too, are the earthwork remains of a fort used both in the Neolithic and Iron Ages. Cooper's Hill, southeast of Gloucester, is an almost sheer slope amid beautiful woodland.

On the slopes of the Cotswold escarpment near Brockworth is Witcombe; in the vicinity are the remains of a Roman villa in a peaceful setting close to woodland.

Looking across to the distinctive scarp of Cleeve Hill from Woodmancote

CHEESE ROLLING

This strange annual ritual takes place every Spring Bank Holiday Monday on Cooper's Hill, just outside the village of Brockworth, near Gloucester. Whilst its precise origins are obscure, it is thought that in its current form it dates back to the 16th century. The brave competitors line up across the crown of what is an exceptionally steep hill (1-in-3) next to a maypole-like flagstaff. A man dressed in a white coat and top hat launches the cheeses down the slope, to be pursued hell for leather by the racers, whose task it is to retrieve one of the cheeses before it reaches the bottom. Anyone who does so, and success is rare, may keep the cheese. Concerns about safety have led to attempts to suppress the event. There is, however, local determination to ensure its survival.

Fine Views and Quiet Villages

A pretty walk that is ideal for those staying in or near
Cheltenham with little time to explore the area.
Mostly field paths and tracks. A lovely summer walk.

Time: 1¾ hours. Distance: 3¾ miles (6km).
Location: 6 miles (9.7km) southeast of Cheltenham.
Start: Kilkenny viewpoint car park, located on the A436 near
Dowdeswell.
(OS grid ref: SP004186.)
OS Maps: Outdoor Leisure 45 (The Cotswolds) 1:25,000.
Explorer 179 (Gloucester, Cheltenham & Stroud) 1:25,000.
See Key to Walks on page 121.

ROUTE DIRECTIONS

From the **Kilkenny**
viewpoint, cross the main
road and go through a
waymarked gate, then keep
to the left-hand edge of two
fields, walking downhill to a
gate and lane.

Turn left, pass an arrowed
path on the right, and gently
climb along a track towards
Castle Barn Farm. Shortly,
turn right on to a rough track
beside a stone wall and soon
follow it between dense
hedges to a junction of tracks
at the edge of a field. Enter
the field, keep to its left-hand
flank to the corner (can be

overgrown), and locate a
short passage to reach a
swing gate near a cottage.
Proceed through a further
gate into a field, from where
there are open views to
Dowdeswell Reservoir and
Rossley Gate away to your
left and Lower Dowdeswell to
the right. Head downhill
towards woodland, keep to
the right of two trees in the
centre of the field, to reach a
gate at the base of the field.
Keep ahead through thin
woodland to cross a stile and
go up a slope, with a pond
and a tennis court to the left.
Continue to a gate situated

to the right of a large house.
Enter a paddock-like area,
with a church in view ahead
to your right, and continue
ahead, crossing a track to a
gate. Join a gravel drive to the
left of an old barn and shortly
turn right on to a road,
following the grass bank. Pass
the church at **Lower
Dowdeswell** (well worth a
visit), and after 200 yards
(183m), turn left on to a track
beside some cottages. Remain
on the track, pass to the left
of a cottage and go through a
bushy area into a field. Go
straight ahead and keep to
the right-hand edge of the
field, eventually reaching a
stile and lane to the left of a
raised grassy strip. Turn right,
continue to pass a burial
ground, then keep ahead over
a crossroads by a barn, and
soon turn right into **Upper
Dowdeswell**.

Pass through the village,
the metalled lane becoming a
hedged track beyond Upper
Dowdeswell Manor. Keep to
the track, the Kilkenny mast
can be seen on the left, and
shortly pass through a gate on
the left to retrace your
outward route across fields to
the A436 and the car park.

*The walk sets out from the
Kilkenny viewpoint near
Dowdeswell*

POINTS OF INTEREST

Kilkenny

A well known viewpoint offering a panorama from the Cotswold escarpment to Cleeve Hill, and northwards across the Severn Vale to the Malverns.

Rossley Gate

The 15th-century half-timbered house opposite Dowdeswell Reservoir originally stood at the corner of Arle Avenue and Gloucester Road in Cheltenham. It was purchased for £500 by Cecil Coxwell Rogers, who moved it to its present site in 1929, to become the gatehouse of Rossley Manor.

Lower Dowdeswell

A small village whose name derives from a Saxon chief named Dodo. The church, next to a Tudor farmhouse, is well worth a visit. It has an impressive tower, complete with dovecots, and contains two mid-19th-century galleries, one for the manor, the other for the

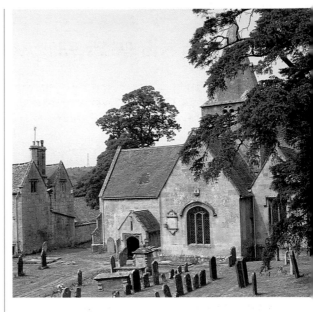

rectory. There is also a handsome 18th-century monument on the chancel wall and a 16th-century brass of a priest.

Upper Dowdeswell

The village consists of two rows of cottages leading up

Church and farmhouse sit side by side in Lower Dowdeswell

to Upper Dowdeswell Manor, which dates back to the 16th century, and is now divided into a number of households.

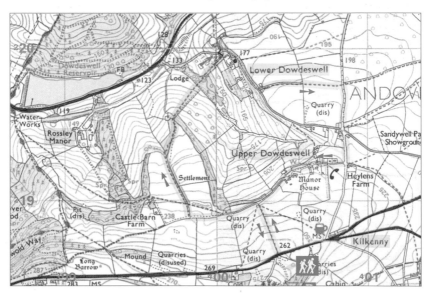

Once an important coaching stop, Moreton-in-Marsh has made way for a gentler holiday traffic

THE FOUR SHIRES STONE

The Four Shires Stone, just to the east of Moreton, is a striking 18th-century monolith surmounted by a sundial and a ball. It marks the original point of conjunction of the counties of Gloucestershire, Oxfordshire, Warwickshire and Worcestershire.

MORETON-IN-MARSH Gloucestershire Map ref SP2032

A bustling market town strung along the Fosse Way, Moreton is very much a roadside town, although its importance also depends on the fact that it has, uniquely in the area, a railway station; the railway arrived in 1843. Prior to the railway, the Stratford and Moreton Tramway, opened in 1826, was an ambitious attempt to link London with the Midlands, and before that, in the coaching era, Moreton was an important stop between London, Oxford, Worcester and Hereford.

Moreton is a place for wandering, particularly on a Tuesday when the weekly market swings into action in the vicinity of the Redesdale Market Hall built in 1887 in Tudor style. The 16th-century Curfew Tower on the corner of Oxford Street was used as recently as 1860 and has a bell dated 1633. Beneath is the town lock-up and a board listing the market tolls of 1905. Just outside the town, on the Broadway Road, is the Wellington Aviation Museum and Art Gallery.

In the vicinity of Moreton are a number of villages worth visiting by car or on foot. Bourton-on-the-Hill climbs the road to Broadway and has a nice pub, a 16th-century tithe barn, and a handsome church with a Winchester bushel and peck (standard measures dating from 1587). Bourton House Gardens are open to visitors.

Bourton's near neighbour is Sezincote, the extraordinary early 19th-century house built in Indian style for Samuel Pepys Cockerell, worth, at the very least, a stroll by. Cockerell's brother, Charles, architect of Sezincote, is buried in the attractive church at Longborough, the neighbouring village.

Batsford, northwest of Moreton is an estate village with a Victorian church containing some excellent monuments whilst Batsford Park has an arboretum and a falconry centre.

THE RISSINGTONS Gloucestershire Map ref SP1917

The Rissingtons, of which there are three, lie southeast of Bourton-on-the-Water. Great Rissington has a handsome 17th-century manor house and a church with some interesting memorials. Little Rissington, on the slope of the Windrush Valley, overlooks gravel pits, now sanctuaries for birds, close to Bourton. Wyck Rissington, its 17th- and 18th-century cottages built about a wide green and village pond, is the loveliest of the three. From the 18th century it formed part of the Wyck Hill estate, until the 1930s when the depression forced it to be sold. In the church, which, like several near the Fosse Way is dedicated to St Laurence who was martyred in Rome in AD 257, there is some 14th-century stained glass and Flemish wooden plaques dating from the 16th century. Gustav Holst, the composer born in Cheltenham, was organist here in 1892 when only 17.

THE SLAUGHTERS Gloucestershire Map ref SP1523
These two villages with unlikely names are, like Bourton-on-the-Water, synonymous with the Cotswolds. Upper Slaughter, partly clustered around the fine Elizabethan manor and the church, is the more pastoral of the two. Beyond the church, which contains a monument to F E Witts, 19th-century rector and lord of the manor, who wrote *Diary of a Cotswold Parson*, the scene is absurdly picturesque – the forded River Eye bubbles in the shade of an oak tree below some wonderful stone cottages.

Lower Slaughter, about a half-mile (0.8km) walk away, is somewhat different in character. The River Eye is spanned, as at Bourton, by a number of flattish footbridges. The 19th century corn mill, with its redundant waterwheel and steam chimney, is an unusual feature, although there has been a mill on the site since at least the time of the Domesday Book. It has been restored in order to demonstrate the workings of a Victorian flour mill; among the collection of artefacts is one of only three unused millstones left in the country.

THE VICARS' DREAM
Although the little village of Wyck Rissington is associated with Gustav Holst (his first professional engagement was here – he lived at the last cottage on the left along the road that goes towards the Fosse Way), it is also noted for something that is no longer here. After World War II the vicar had a dream in which he saw crowds in a maze whilst an invisible supervisor directed its construction. The vicar apparently saw this as a sign, and a symbol of a spiritual pilgrimage, spending some years in building a maze of considerable proportions in the vicarage garden which was opened to the public on Coronation Day in 1953. The maze has now gone but there remains a memorial wall-tablet to its creator, Canon Harry Cheales.

The clear waters of the Eye broaden at the ford, Upper Slaughter

An Exotic Stately Home

Starting from the attractive hillside village of Bourton-on-the-Hill, the less famous cousin of Bourton-on-the-Water, this short, level walk explores good field paths near the stately home of Sezincote.

Time: 1¾ hours. Distance: 3 miles (4.8km).
Location: 2 miles (3.2km) west of Moreton-in-Marsh.
Start: Bourton-on-the-Hill, on the A44 between Chipping Norton and Broadway. Car park (not signed) behind the old school building off the main street.
(OS grid ref: SP175325.)
OS Map: Outdoor Leisure 45 (The Cotswolds) 1:25,000.
See Key to Walks on page 121.

ROUTE DIRECTIONS

In **Bourton-on-the-Hill**, take the lane by the car park away from the main road, turn left, then shortly follow the waymarked walled track right to a gate. Proceed ahead alongside a stone wall to a gate, cross a field to a further gate and continue through the next pasture to a stile in a wooden fence. Maintain direction to a kissing gate, pass through a band of trees to another gate, then head across a field between spinneys, with the cupola of **Sezincote House** coming into view.

Cross an estate road, then descend a slope towards woodland. At the bottom pass to the right of a wooden fence and head for two gates in quick succession, then go between two ponds into a meadow. To your right is the incongruous 'Indian palace' of Sezincote Manor. Proceed across the field to a gate by a water trough, then head uphill, bearing slightly right to another gate by stone walls in the top right-hand corner of the field.

Turn left on to a road (views to Longborough on the right), pass a cottage and go through two gateways, before bearing left and right towards Upper Rye Farm. Pass the farm entrance on the left and head towards a black barn, keeping right of a fence to a gate, then turn sharp left to pass between the barn and farmhouse.

Continue through a gate by a cattle grid then, immediately beyond a second grid, climb a stile on your left. Keep left-handed beside a ditch, cross a footbridge and bear sharp right along the field edge, with Bourton visible ahead. Climb a stile in the top right corner and follow the path through trees beside a stream, as it bears left to a stile. Maintain course over a further field to a stile

Well-screened cottages in the charming village of Bourton-on-the-Hill

and lane. Cross the stile opposite, proceed along the field edge to a tree, then turn right along a rough path between hedges.

Shortly, turn left along a hedge and head uphill through a series of gates and fields to reach the outward path, which leads you back to the church in Bourton-on-the-Hill and the car park.

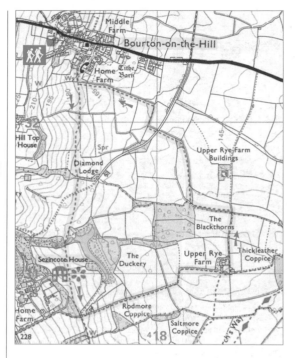

POINTS OF INTEREST

Bourton-on-the-Hill
Bourton is an attractive hillside village which lies just below the high wolds. The church dates from Norman times and some of the original, stolid pillars in local stone still stand to one side of the nave. Here, too, is the Winchester bushel and peck – weight standards which date from the reign of Elizabeth I.

The fine tithe barn, near by, is marked in the name of one Richard Palmer who was linked by marriage to the Overbury family. Sir Thomas Overbury was murdered in the Tower of London in 1613 by the slow administration of poison; he had been imprisoned by Lady Essex because he opposed the marriage between her and Robert Carr, favourite of James I. He died after living in agony for months and it was only some years later that the truth emerged.

Sezincote Manor
This transplant from India dates back to the turn of the 19th century when Sir Charles Cockerell, who made his fortune with the East India Company, had the manor built by his architect brother, Thomas Daniell, a well known painter of Indian scenes, and Humphry Repton. Some people believe that the great Nash had a hand in its design, too.

The Prince Regent, who visited in 1807, was inspired to create Brighton Pavilion. The house was often visited by the poet Sir John Betjeman who mentions Sezincote Manor in one of his poems.

Yellow waymark arrows indicate the path

A fantastical collection of musical instruments at Snowshill Manor, including two serpents

CHARLES 'SCHEMER' KEYTE
A Snowshill man, Charles 'Schemer' Keyte, is sometimes accredited the inventor of the sewing machine. His machine, which he invented in Rose Cottage in 1842, is now exhibited in the Science Museum in London, and a cumbersome contraption it certainly seems. The Keyte family were well-known craftsmen in the Snowshill area for centuries. A bell was donated to Campden church by a Captain Thomas Keyte in 1683 and another member of the family was a wheelwright in the18th century.

SNOWSHILL Gloucestershire Map ref SP0933
Pronounced, according to some, 'Snowzzle', or even 'Snozzle', this charming and comparatively remote village is famous, above all, for Snowshill Manor, a National Trust property from the Tudor period that once belonged to the wealthy and eccentric sugar plantation owner, Charles Wade. An ardent collector of anything that was crafted, he filled the manor house with his finds, living, meanwhile, in the Priest's House in the lovely terraced garden, without any comforts or conveniences and sleeping in an old Tudor bed. The fame of Snowshill Manor travelled far and wide, so that eminent people – John Buchan, John Betjeman, J B Priestley, and Queen Mary who apparently said that the finest thing in the house was Charles Wade – were frequent visitors.

Truly Snowshill Manor is one of the most astonishing and absorbing museums possible; of interest, with its Japanese armour, farm implements, musical instruments, clocks and toys – to name but a few – to all but the most hardened detractor of museums.

STANTON Gloucestershire SP0634
A village of quite ridiculous perfection, Stanton's fine collection of farmhouses and cottages, most of which were built in the 17th century, the golden period of Cotswold vernacular architecture, seems to have been preserved in aspic; and indeed it is regularly used as the backdrop for period films. It owes its peculiar 'frozen-in-time' quality to the man who bought much of the village before World War I, the architect Sir Philip Stott,

who hailed from Oldham in Lancashire.

Living in Stanton Court, he determined to restore Stanton. This he did, introducing modern conveniences in the process, but ensuring by covenant that the more unsightly features of the 20th century were not to disfigure the village. A place to stroll around (making use of the car park around the corner of the Broadway road), Stanton's church, St Michael's, is delightful and well worth a visit. It boasts a handsomely slender spire, has a number of 12th-century features in the north arcade and also two pulpits, one 14th century, one Jacobean. It also has some 15th-century stained glass which came from Hailes Abbey near Winchcombe. The village has a fine pub at its far end, the Mount Inn, in the shadow of Shenbarrow Hill, with its Iron-Age earthworks and magnificent views.

STANWAY Gloucestershire Map ref SP0632

No more, really, than a hamlet, Stanway is dominated by Stanway House and its quite beautiful gatehouse. Just off the B4077 Stow road, Stanway House is reached by passing the striking St George and Dragon, a bronze war memorial by Alexander Fisher on a plinth by Sir Philip Stott, 'saviour' of nearby Stanton.

For a long time the 17th-century gatehouse was thought to be by Inigo Jones, a theory that has been superseded by the belief that it is the work of Timothy Strong, the mason from the Barringtons whose family worked with Sir Christopher Wren on St Paul's Cathedral. The glow of the stone is breathtaking, particularly at sunset.

The house itself, a Jacobean building with medieval origins, has changed hands only once in over a thousand years and definitely warrants a visit. Still inhabited by the owner, Lord Niedpath, whose aristocratic presence is much in evidence, the house wears an attractively lived-in aspect; and although it contains many items of interest and value, some unique, a less fossilised atmosphere is hard to imagine.

In the grounds there is a magnificent tithe barn built in about 1370; today it is a beautiful setting for musical events and flower shows. The old water cascade, which used to gush down steps from a huge pyramid behind the house, is eventually to be reactivated after many years disuse. The old brewhouse has sprung to life again producing a beer called Stanway, apparently pronounced 'Stanny'. Brewed on a Monday, when the air about Stanway becomes yeasty, the beer is gradually spreading into local pubs.

Next to the house is the church, similarly cloaked in refulgent gold, and with a Jacobean pulpit. Near by is a thatched wooden cricket pavilion, presented to the village by J M Barrie, author of *Peter Pan*. Barrie, a keen cricketer, was a frequent visitor to Stanway in the early years of the 20th century.

JOHN WESLEY AND STANTON

The 18th-century preacher John Wesley was a regular visitor to Stanton where he stayed with his friends, the family of the Reverend Lionel Kirkham. John Wesley often preached in the church here.

TINKERBELL

It is sometimes said, and it may be true, that the inspiration to create the character of the fairy Tinkerbell came to J M Barrie when he saw a moonbeam strike the wall of his bedroom during a sojourn at Stanway.

Scallop shells on the 17th-century gatehouse are a reminder of the Jacobean builders of Stanway House

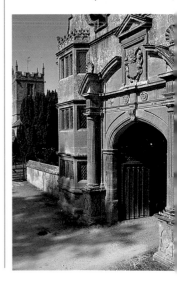

The restored market cross marks the heart of Stow-on-the-Wold

WINDY WOLDS
A little rhyme illustrates perfectly Stow's windswept reputation, according to which, of the four elements, only air prospered:

'Stow on the Wold
Where the wind blows cold
And the cooks can't roast their dinners.'

OUR LIVING AGRICULTURAL HERITAGE
At the Cotswold Farm Park, the home of rare breeds conservation, there are nearly 50 breeding flocks and herds of ancient breeds of British cattle, horses, pigs, sheep, goats, poultry and waterfowl. Newborn lambs and goat kids can be seen in April, spring calves in May, foals in June and piglets throughout the year.

STOW-ON-THE-WOLD Gloucestershire Map ref SP1925
This windswept town, the highest in the Cotswolds, is at the meeting point of eight roads, and lies on the Roman Fosse Way, midway between Bourton and Moreton. At its heart is the old market square, surrounded by attractive pubs and coaching inns, shops and restaurants, for Stow's main claim to fame was as a prosperous and busy market town.

The square is not typical of the Cotswolds – its even, rectangular shape is more reminiscent of an Italian piazza, but without the arcades. Perhaps its exposed position on the wolds dictated its shape, to protect market traders from the wind. Leading into the square are a number of walled alleys or 'tures' which it is thought once served the purpose of directing the sheep towards the market place. The old stocks are still in place on the remains of the green in a corner of the square, whilst in the centre stands the Victorian St Edward's Hall, whose massive presence tends to overpower the more modest lines of the other buildings. Just to the south of the Hall is the medieval market cross, placed there as an appeal to the religious conscience of traders in their commercial dealings.

Overlooking the square is the imposing Norman church of St Edward which in 1646 played host to 1,000 Royalist prisoners following the final battle of the Civil War, which was fought in the vicinity of neighbouring Donnington. Its north door is picturesquely framed by a pair of tree trunks whilst just outside the churchyard, on Church Street, is Stow's 17th-century school, now a masonic hall.

The Royalist pub, at the junction of Park Street and Digbeth Street which runs southeast from the square, claims to be the oldest in the county; unlike the many other claimants for this title, remains of wooden beams have been discovered here which, scientific tests prove, were in place a thousand years ago.

There are a number of villages in the vicinity of Stow that are worth visiting. A 45-minute walk (or a short drive) from Stow to the north is Broadwell, built around a large green with a ford and overlooked by a fine pub, the Fox. To the west are the Swells, Lower and Upper. In Lower Swell the unusual design of Spa Cottages is a reminder of a chalybeate spring which was discovered here in 1807. It was hoped that the discovery would encourage visitors to come and take the waters, according to the fashion of the time, but the project foundered. At Upper Swell the road crosses a narrow 18th-century bridge near a mill, complete with a wheel. Also to the west of Stow is the Cotswold Farm Park, a fascinating collection of rare British breeds of pigs, sheep, cattle and horses in a typical Cotswold farm setting. The aim of the farm is to ensure the survival of these old breeds and a visit is to be recommended.

THE COTSWOLD WAY
The Cotswold Way is a challenging long-distance footpath of about 90 miles (144km), between Bath and Chipping Campden. It takes about nine days to complete if attempted in one go, otherwise it is possible to walk short sections of the route.

Decorative window design on Spa Cottages at Lower (or Nether) Swell

VINEYARDS AND TOBACCO
The slopes around
Winchcombe were put to a
number of uses apart from
nourishing sheep. The monks
from the abbey made wine,
whilst tobacco was an
important crop for some
decades after the Dissolution
of the Monasteries until the
government felt that the
competition did not help the
new colony of Virginia and
proscribed its cultivation.

WINCHCOMBE Gloucestershire Map ref SP0228
The old capital of the Saxon kingdom of Mercia,
Winchcombe is a town of considerable interest, with
several legacies of its past that deserve investigation.
During the Middle Ages there was an important abbey
here, much frequented by pilgrims who came to worship
at the burial place of the martyred Prince Kenelm.
Dissolved on Christmas Eve 1539, all that remains of the
abbey is the wall on one side of Abbey Terrace (behind
which is now private property) and the abbey church,
now Winchcombe parish church. The handsome church,
of 1465–8, owes its present form to the wealth of local
woolmen and of particular note here are the 40 or so
gargoyles, 'the Winchcombe Worthies', that adorn the
exterior, apparently representing unpopular monks, an
indication of general dissatisfaction with the abbey at
the time. Within is a stone coffin that purports to have
contained the body of St Kenelm, and also a piece of
embroidery attributed in part to Katherine of Aragon,
Henry VIII's first wife.

Along the main street are an assortment of interesting
buildings (including the fine Jacobean old school on
Abbey Terrace), as well as two small museums – the
Railway Museum, with a fascinating collection of
memorabilia, and the Winchcombe Museum in the town
hall, next to the Tourist Information Centre, with a
collection of police uniforms and finds from Belas Knap
Neolithic barrow (see page 37).

Gloucestershire, strangely in view of its location close
to Wales, has very few castles; but Sudeley, the entrance
to which is down Vineyard Street, is superb. Little
remains of the original medieval castle, but of the 15th-
century reconstruction undertaken by Ralph Botelar, St
Mary's Chapel, the ruined banqueting hall, the tithe
barn and the Portmare Tower are extant.

During its Tudor and Elizabethan heyday, Sudeley was
a place of eminence. Its owner, the ambitious Thomas

*Winchcombe lies beneath
the scarp of Cleeve Hill*

A pop-eyed gargoyle, one of the 'Winchcombe Worthies', on the parish church

Seymour, Lord High Admiral of England, eventually married Catherine Parr, the only one of Henry VIII's wives to survive him. She died here following childbirth and is buried in the chapel. Later, Queen Elizabeth I was to visit the castle on three occasions. A Royalist stronghold during the Civil War, the castle was severely damaged in 1644 and partially demolished in 1648.

In the 19th century the estate was purchased by the Dent brothers, well known for their glove-making business. They began restoration of the castle but when it passed to their nephew, it was his wife, Emma Dent-Brocklehurst, an avid collector of anything linked to the castle, who ensured its present immaculate state. Still privately owned, the castle is set in wonderful ornamental gardens, beautifully sited beneath the Cotswold escarpment; within is a remarkable collection of furniture and paintings, all displayed with a studied nonchalance that is a delight.

Close to Winchcombe are a number of places worth visiting. A 45-minute walk, or a short drive, can take you to Belas Knap, one of the best preserved Neolithic barrows in the country and from where there are lovely views back across Sudeley and Winchcombe. At Toddington you can take a ride on a steam train along a restored part of the Honeybourne Line (Gloucestershire–Warwickshire Railway) which, it is planned, will eventually be reopened back to Cheltenham. The remains of Hailes Abbey a short drive to the northeast, just off the Stow road, evoke the romance of the Middle Ages, whilst Hailes parish church, near by, is of particular interest with its painted medieval tiles.

MAJESTIC GARDENS
Sudeley Castle has eight delightful gardens where visitors can wander through splendid avenues of trees, shrubs, yew hedges and old-fashioned roses. Also within the grounds are a wildfowl sanctuary, an exhibition centre, a plant centre, picnic area and a shop and restaurant. Special events, including a game fair, craft shows and musical evenings are held in the grounds throughout the year.

The Northern Cotswolds

Leisure Information

Places of Interest

Shopping

Sports, Activities and the

Outdoors

Annual Events and Customs

✔ Checklist

Leisure Information

TOURIST INFORMATION CENTRES

Broadway
1 Cotswold Court. Tel: 01386 852937 (seasonal).
Chipping Campden
High Street.
Tel: 01386 841206.
Moreton-in-Marsh
Council Offices, High Street. Tel: 01608 650881. Information point only, bookings cannot be made.
Stow-on-the-Wold
Hollis House, The Square.
Tel: 01451 831082.

Winchcombe
The Town Hall, High Street.
Tel: 01242 602925 (seasonal).

OTHER INFORMATION

English Heritage
29 Queen Square, Bristol.
Tel: 0117 975 0700
www.english-heritage.org.uk
National Trust
Severn Region, Mythe End House, Tewkesbury. Tel: 01684 850051.
www.nationaltrust.org.uk

Parts of lovely Sudeley Castle were restored by George Gilbert Scott

Parking
Park with care in small villages which have no car parks, do not block driveways or field entrances. If you park on the road, allow room for vehicles, including lorries, to pass.

ORDNANCE SURVEY MAPS

Landranger 1:50,000 Sheets 150, 151, 163. Outdoor Leisure 1:25,000 Sheet 45

Places of Interest

There will be an admission charge at the following places of interest unless otherwise stated.
Batsford Arboretum
Batsford Park, Moreton-in-Marsh. Tel: 01386 701441.
Open Mar–Nov, daily.
Birdland
Rissington Road, Bourton-on-the-Water. Tel: 01451 820480.
Open all year, daily.
Bourton House Gardens
Bourton-on-the-Hill. Tel: 01386 700121. Open May–Oct, Thu, Fri & Bank Hol Sun 10–5.
Bredon Tithe Barn
Bredon. Tel: 01684 850051.
Open Apr–Nov, certain days.
Broadway Tower Country Park
Broadway. Tel: 01386 852390.

Open Apr–Oct, daily.
Cotswold Falconry Centre
Batsford Park, Moreton-in-
Marsh. Tel: 01386 701043.
Open Mar–Oct, daily.
Cotswold Farm Park
Guiting Power. Tel: 01451
850307. Open Apr–Oct, daily.
**Cotswold Motor Museum,
Toy Collection and Village
Life Exhibition**
The Old Mill, Bourton-on-the-
Water. Tel: 01451 821255.
Open Feb–Nov, daily.
Cotswold Perfumery
Victoria Street, Bourton on the
Water. Tel: 01451 820698.
Open all year, daily.
Folly Farm Waterfowl
Notgrove, Bourton-on-the-
Water. Tel: 01451 820285.
Open all year, daily.
**Gloucestershire and
Warwickshire Railway**
Toddington Station,
Winchcombe. Tel: 01242
621405. Open daily; steam
services at weekends and Bank
Hols, mid-Mar to mid-Oct, also
mid-week specials in summer.
Hailes Abbey
Winchcombe. Tel: 01242
602398. Open Easter or
Apr–Oct, daily; Nov–Easter,
weekends.
Hidcote Manor Garden
Mickleton. Tel: 01684 855370.
Open Apr–Oct, most days.

House open Tue in Jun &Jul.
Kiftsgate Court Garden
Mickleton. Tel: 01386 438777.
Open Apr–Sep, some days.
Model Railway Exhibition
Box Bush, High Street, Bourton-
on-the-Water. Tel: 01451
820686. Open Apr–Sep daily,
Oct–Mar, weekends only.
Model Village
Old New Inn, Main Street,
Bourton-on-the-Water.
Tel: 01451 820467. Open all
year, daily.
Old Mill Museum
Mill Lane, Lower Slaughter.
Tel: 01451 820052. Open all
year, daily.
Sezincote
Moreton-in-Marsh. Tel: 01386
700444. Open: house May–Jul
and Sep: some afternoons.
Gardens: Jan–Nov, some
afternoons.
Snowshill Manor
Tel: 01386 852410. Open
Apr–Oct, most afternoons.
Stanway House
Tel: 01386 584469. Open
Aug–Sep, some afternoons.
Sudeley Castle and Gardens
Winchcombe. Tel: 01242
602308. Open Mar–Oct, daily.
**Wellington Aviation
Museum & Art Gallery**
Broadway Road, Moreton-in-
Marsh. Tel: 01608 650323.
Open all year, most days.

Kiftsgate Court Garden

**Winchcombe Folk and
Police Museum**
Old Town Hall, Winchcombe.
Tel. 01242 609151. Open
Apr–Oct, most days.
Winchcombe Pottery
Broadway Road. Tel: 01242
602462. Open all year, most
days.

SPECIAL INTEREST FOR CHILDREN

The following places may be of
interest to visitors with children.
Unless otherwise stated, there
will be an admission charge.
**Broadway Tower Country
Park**
Broadway. Tel: 01386 852390.
Exhibitions, animals, magnificent
views. Open Apr–Oct, daily.
Folly Farm Waterfowl
Notgrove, Bourton-on-the-
Water. Tel: 01451 820285.
Waterfowl, hand-reared pets'
area. Open all year, daily.
Gifford Circus
This Gloucestershire-based
1930s-style circus tours
Cotswold villages in summer.
Tel: 07818 058384.
Model Village
Old New Inn, Main Street,
Bourton-on-the-Water.
Tel: 01451 820467. Open all
year, daily.

Shopping

In most of the villages featured in the gazetteer, shopping will be confined to the post office and the village shop; some of the better known villages have tourist shops. Larger villages like Moreton, Stow and Winchcombe have a variety of general and antiques shops.
Moreton-in-Marsh
Market in town centre, Tue.

LOCAL SPECIALITIES

Pottery
Conderton Pottery, Conderton. Tel: 01386 89387.
Winchcombe Pottery, Broadway Road, Winchcombe. Tel: 01242 602462.
Silk Printing
Silk printing at Beckford Silk, Ashton Road, near Tewkesbury. Tel: 01386 881507.
Silverware
David Hart, Silversmiths, Sheep Street, Chipping Campden. Tel: 01386 841100.

Sports, Activities and the Outdoors

ANGLING

Although most fishing is private in the area, permits can be arranged through some hotels.
Aston Magna Pool
near Moreton. Day permits are available from Batsford Estate Office. Tel: 01608 650425 (evenings only).

The former estate village of Stanton is carefully preserved

ARCHERY

Moreton-in-Marsh
Rob Ireland Country Crafts and Leisure, Lower Lemington. Tel: 01608 650413.

CLAY PIGEON SHOOTING

Coberley
Chatcombe Estate Shooting School, Chatcombe, Coberley. Tel: 01242 870391.
Moreton-in-Marsh
Rob Ireland Country Crafts and Leisure, Lower Lemington. Tel: 01608 650413.

COUNTRY PARKS AND NATURE RESERVES

Broadway Tower Country Park, Broadway. Tel: 01386 852390. Views from observation room in tower. Open Apr–Oct, daily. Crickley Hill, near Leckhampton.

CYCLING

Country Lanes Cycle Hire, Moreton Railway Station, Moreton-in-Marsh. Tel: 01608 650065.

GOLF COURSES

Broadway
Broadway Golf Course, Willersley Hill. Tel: 01386 853683.
Cleeve Hill
Cleeve Hill Golf Course, near Prestbury. Tel: 01242 672025/672592.

Naunton
Naunton Downs Golf Club, Stow Road. Tel: 01451 850090.
Ullenwood
Cotswold Hills Golf Course. Tel: 01242 515264.

GUIDED WALKS

Cotswolds Walking Holidays Ltd, 10 Royal Parade, Bayshill Road, Cheltenham. Tel: 01242 254353, Fax: 01242 518888. Organised walking holidays in the area, weekend breaks, village to village walks.
The Voluntary Wardens, part of the Cotswold Countryside Service, arrange guided walks. Tel: 01452 425674.

HILL-CLIMBING

The motor speed hill-climbs at Prescott, 2 miles (3.2km) west of Winchcombe, are held about six times a year. Operated by the Bugatti Owners' Club. Tel: 01242 673136.

Annual Events and Customs

Chipping Campden
Dover's Hill Olympick Games and Scuttlebrook Wake. Spring Bank Holiday.
Cooper's Hill
Cheese Rolling, Spring Bank Holiday Monday.
Cranham
Annual Feast and Ox Roast, August.
Guiting Power
Festival of Music and Arts, July.
Moreton-in-Marsh
Agricultural Show, September.
Winchcombe
Sudeley Castle stages various events from April to October, including musical events and crafts fairs. Tel: 01242 602308

The checklists give details of just some of the facilities within the area covered by this guide. Further information can be obtained from Tourist Information Centres.

The Severn Vale and the Vale of Berkeley

The Severn Vale lies between the Cotswold escarpment and the River Severn, Britain's longest river; along the banks of the Severn are the flat fertile lands of the Vale of Berkeley. The Severn Vale, with its brick houses and half-timbered cottages, is quite different in character from the sugared stone villages of the wolds, yet wold and vale are closely linked – they both, to a large extent, belong to Gloucestershire and many of the historical events that have shaped the county have taken place in the towns of the vale and wold and, consequently, they are almost inseparable.

The Boat Inn, a hostelry for almost 200 years

ASHLEWORTH Gloucestershire Map ref SO8125
Although this little village lies on the west bank of the Severn, it deserves a mention. It is noted for its huge 125-foot (38m) tithe barn and its once fortified manor house, Ashleworth Court, both of which, along with the church, are close to the water; the rest of the village is built well away from possible floods.

On the river bank itself is the Boat Inn, which has been run by the same family since its construction at the beginning of the 19th century. The family in question, the Jelfs, were granted the ferry rights here over 300 years ago when a Mr Jelf rowed Charles I across the river in 1643 as he fled the Siege of Gloucester.

THE SEVERN BORE
The Severn Bore, the wave that travels along the lower reaches of the river, can be up to 9 feet (just under 3m) high. It is caused by the tidal movements of the Bristol Channel and the Severn Estuary which experiences one of the greatest tidal ranges in the world. At low tide the water recedes to leave an extensive area of mudflats which are rapidly covered by the returning tide. The local press reports on its movements and among the best vantage points are Elmore and Minsterworth. A leaflet predicting the relative quality of the Bore may be obtained from Tourist Information Centres.

Along the Romantic Road

This drive of some 60 miles (96.6km), beginning and
ending in the splendidly-preserved Regency town of
Cheltenham, will take you through some delightful, but
lesser-known areas of the Cotswolds.

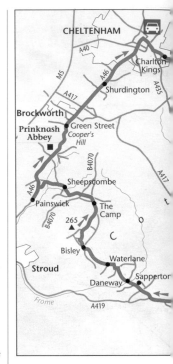

ROUTE DIRECTIONS

See Key to Car Tours on page 120.
From Cheltenham take the A40 London road to pass through Charlton Kings, where Lewis Carroll was inspired to write *Alice Through the Looking Glass*, and then pass by Dowdeswell Reservoir, the largest stretch of water in Gloucestershire. Soon turn right to Dowdeswell, to climb fairly steeply up the Cotswold escarpment. Follow this country lane, crossing three sets of crossroads, towards Withington. Go through the village, with its large monastery church, pass the Mill Inn and continue until a sign indicates **Chedworth Villa** and Yanworth. Follow a still narrower country lane around the solitary manor farmhouse of Cassey Compton, until the road breaks off for the Roman villa, considered to be the finest in the country.

After visiting the villa, pass through Yanworth and head for Northleach. Drive along the High Street and soon after turn left for Farmington. Go through the village of Farmington and follow the lanes along the delightfully named Windrush Valley and its quiet villages of Sherborne (Sherborne House is said to be haunted by a hunchback Royalist) and Windrush. Turn right for Little Barrington. Pass through Little Barrington, with its pretty post office and large green – this is the heart of stone-producing country and once home of Thomas Strong, master mason for St

Paul's Cathedral. Continue to the A40 and turn left.

Bypass Burford for now by continuing across a round-about and then, after a mile (1.6km), turn left and then right for Widford and then Swinbrook, a pretty village associated with the Mitford sisters, two of whom are buried in the churchyard. Leave Swinbrook and fork left for Fulbrook. Drive through to a junction and turn left to cross a medieval bridge into Burford, one of the loveliest of Cotswold villages, which slopes down to the Windrush and has a plethora of shops, inns and delightful houses. Drive up the sloping main street to the roundabout on the A40 and go straight across on the A361 in the

***The River Coln flows through
tranquil meadows at Cassey
Compton***

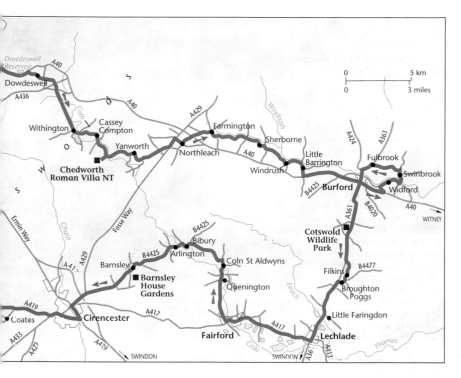

direction of Lechlade, pausing to stop at Filkins and its working woollen mill.

Lechlade is the meeting point of the Thames, the Coln and the Leach. From Lechlade turn right along the A417 to Fairford, whose church contains the finest set of medieval stained glass in England. Cross the river and turn right for Quenington and thence to Coln St Aldwyns. Go through the village and then, near where parkland comes to an end on the right, turn left for Bibury, famously described by William Morris as 'the most beautiful village in the Cotswolds'. From Bibury take the B4425, passing through Barnsley (Barnsley House Gardens, designed by Rosemary Verey, are open to the public), to Cirencester. In Roman times the town was second in importance only to London; it has a fine museum,

'wool' church and magnificent landscaped park.

Take the A419 towards Stroud, looking for a small road on the right in the direction of Sapperton after about 3 miles (4.8km). Follow this road to Daneway where the pub marks the entrance to the Thames and Severn Canal Tunnel. From here take the road, on a corner on the left, which climbs up towards Bisley. To get there fork left, then right and follow the road through Waterlane to come to a junction at a main road just outside Bisley. Cross carefully and go down to the main thoroughfare of this handsome village. Turn right, then left opposite the post office.

Pass the Bear Inn and soon turn right towards The Camp and Birdlip. Immediately after The Camp turn left at an electricity generator, for Sheepscombe, a pretty village

associated with Laurie Lee and his childhood autobiography *Cider with Rosie*. Cross the B4070 and then fork right for the village, passing the village hall and pub. Use the spire of Painswick church as a landmark and keep on this road until you reach the the A46, where you turn left for Painswick. The 'Queen of the Cotswolds', this is a beautiful, working village with magnificent churchyard. From Painswick, return on the A46 towards Cheltenham. Continue through several miles of beech woodland, passing **Prinknash Abbey**, a modern Benedictine abbey with a pottery, on the left, and Cooper's Hill, scene of the annual Whitsun cheese rolling event, on the right, and then descend to the vale, to continue, via a roundabout, through Shurdington, back to Cheltenham.

Dominating the village, Berkeley Castle offers magnificent views across the gardens to the river

BERKELEY Gloucestershire Map ref ST6899

Gloucestershire is remarkably short on castles. There are only two of note, Sudeley and Berkeley; and whilst Sudeley and its gardens epitomise Renaissance England, Berkeley seems to belong to the mistier, more bellicose Middle Ages. Whilst it is not quite the moated and portcullised castle of fairy tales, Berkeley is an altogether more fortress-like concoction of towers and dense walls, in forbidding, purple stone. It is not surprising, for Berkeley Castle was for centuries the home of one of the region's most powerful families, whose descendants continue to live here as they have done in unbroken line for over 800 years and who opened the castle to the public only in the late 1950s.

The castle domain was granted to the Fitzharding family in 1153 by Henry II from which period most of the current building dates, although there were substantial additions made in the 14th century. Following his deposition in the same year, as a result of his incompetence, Edward II was murdered here in 1327, in the King's Gallery. There is much to enjoy – the dungeons, the Great Hall, the Morning Room with its magnificent medieval ceiling, and a wonderful collection of works of art from all disciplines, including silverware, furniture and tapestries.

In the western wall is the huge breach made by the Parliamentary army during the Civil War, after which the castle was returned to the owners on the condition that the gap was never repaired.

An excellent view can be had of the castle by continuing a short distance beyond the High Street, pass Jumpers Lane on the right (named after the way barges came up Berkeley Pill, a tributary of the Severn, in stages

JENNER'S BALLOON
Edward Jenner was not only an eminent surgeon – he was also the builder of the first balloon to fly over Gloucestershire. He was helped in his enterprise by Frederick Lord Berkeley who allowed him to launch his balloons from the castle's keep tower.

to ride a series of high tides) and look for a stile on the left. Pass into the field and there it is.

Close by is the Church of St Mary, in Early English style with many reminders of the Berkeley dynasty. It is a sign of the times to have to report that it is frequently closed but if you are able to enter you will find some interesting items. Among the wall decorations is a Doom painting (a vision of death to urge the congregation away from the path of sin) above the chancel arch, whilst the Berkeley tombs are just off the chancel. The churchyard is filled with table-top tombs which separate the church from the bell tower built in 1753.

Also a short distance from the castle is the Jenner Museum which is dedicated to the life and work of a local man, Edward Jenner (1749–1823), who discovered the secret of vaccination against smallpox, a disease now officially eradicated. The museum is in the exceptionally handsome Georgian house where he lived. In the garden is the so-called Temple of Vaccinia, where he vaccinated local people free of charge. Jenner is buried in the chancel of the church.

CHELTENHAM Gloucestershire Map ref SO9422
Built against the base of the Cotswold escarpment, overlooked by Cleeve and Leckhampton Hills, Cheltenham calls itself the 'Centre for the Cotswolds', a soubriquet that accurately reflects the town's situation, which is ideal for visiting not only the Cotswolds but also the Severn Vale, the Forest of Dean and the Wye Valley. It is also the scene for several festivals: a Folk Festival in February; the National Hunt Festival when the Gold Cup is run; Jazz in April; the Summer Cricket Festival in the grounds of the Boys' College; the Music Festival in July; and the Literature Festival in October.

Cheltenham is usually associated with the Regency period, when a small market town of comparative insignificance became a fashionable watering hole

DECORATIVE IRONWORK
Cheltenham is noted for its ironwork which decorates many of the early buildings of the town. Distinctive balconies of finely wrought iron adorn many of the elegant buildings, adding a continental atmosphere to the streets and squares. Particularly fine examples are to be found along Oxford Parade, Royal Parade and Suffolk Square.

Perfect symmetry displayed along Cheltenham's outstanding Regency Promenade

HOME OF NATIONAL HUNT RACING

A visit to Cheltenham Racecourse is a 'must' for anyone interested in watching the best chasers and hurdlers in the world. The track is best known for the National Hunt Festival in March, the top three-day meeting of the season which features the Gold Cup and Champion Hurdle and attracts some 50,000 spectators. The Cheltenham Hall of Fame tells the story of the history of the racecourse.

Ornamental caryatids separate the shops along Montpellier Street, adding an air of distinction

following the discovery of minerals in the local water. When George III came here for a cure in 1788 the town's status was secure for the next 100 years or so and the ensuing building boom has left us a town of considerable charm and elegance, of handsome, wide streets lined with Regency style villas and terraces. With one glaring exception, dissonant building has not been permitted, resulting in a town which, despite having the usual share of social problems, retains a veneer that is at the very least aesthetically pleasing.

The town centre is reasonably compact and can easily be explored on foot. The original town ran along the current High Street, now home to many major chain stores and two shopping arcades. The Regency town spread southwards along the Promenade, one of the finest town thoroughfares in the country, now lined with elegant shops. The magnificent terrace at the northern end, built originally to house those coming to take the waters, now houses the Municipal Offices and the Tourist Information Centre. In front is the Neptune Fountain and a statue to Edward Wilson, the Cheltenham botanist who accompanied Captain Robert Scott on his ill-fated expedition to the South Pole.

The Promenade continues gently up, passing the Imperial Garden and the Town Hall on the left, and reaching the imposing, porticoed façade of the Queens Hotel, built on the site of the Imperial Well. The Imperial Well was one of several that were developed to cash in on the spa boom, but by 1837 the owners decided to concentrate on the Montpellier Spa, also theirs, and build a hotel instead.

The road narrows between the shops here. It is worth walking along Queens Circus towards Fauconberg Street, on the right, a short way – on the right is Cheltenham Ladies' College, part of which conceals the original Royal Well; on the left is one of Cheltenham's loveliest streets, Montpellier Street, lined with interesting shops raised

Enjoying an open-air art exhibition in Imperial Square

from the road behind wide pavements. A small alleyway on the left from Montpellier Street leads back towards the main road passing the old Montpellier Arcade to the left and to the right an arch to shops apparently supported by caryatids, armless maidens based on the classical models of the Erechtheion in Athens.

At the top of the road is the Rotunda, now a bank and originally the Montpellier Spa, its design apparently based on the Pantheon in Rome. The interior has been well preserved and is worth a look.

If you have the time there is a lot more Regency architecture to enjoy in the area close to Montpellier, notably in Lansdowne which is just to the west of Montpellier. Southeast will take you to Suffolk Square, just beyond which, along Suffolk Parade and Suffolk Road, are a number of antique and curio shops.

North of the High Street is Pittville and its showpiece, Pittville Pump Rooms. The Pump Rooms constitute a magnificent architectural ensemble, arguably the finest in the town and were designed in 1825–30 by a local man, John Forbes. They were to be the focal point of Joseph Pitt's Pittville Estate, an attempt to create a sort of new town away from the Promenade area. The project never achieved fruition mostly because by the time it got underway in the 1820s, Cheltenham's boom time had passed. Fortunately some part of Pitt's plan was realised and the legacies are the Pump Rooms, Pittville Park with its lake surrounded by villas in an array of fantastic styles, Pittville Lawn, and a pair of squares – Clarence Square and Wellington Square. In the Pump Rooms, often used for concerts and recitals, you can still taste the waters or visit the museum on its upper floor.

The city's art gallery and museum, on Clarence Street, deserves a visit. Whilst the collection as a whole is an eclectic one, there are several areas of specialisation, notably an impressive display of oriental porcelain, an exhibition devoted to the life of Edward Wilson and the work of the 19th-century Arts and Crafts Movement.

Cheltenham's most famous son is the composer Gustav Holst who was born here in 1874. The house where he grew up in Clarence Road is now a museum

TREADING THE BOARDS
Cheltenham still boasts a theatre, the only professional one in Gloucestershire. Unfortunately it is constantly beset with financial problems which is regrettable since it is a handsome building with a considerable history. It was designed by Frank Matcham, the architect responsible for the Coliseum and Palladium in London and when it opened as the New Theatre and Opera House on 1 October 1891, the stage was graced by no lesser star than Lillie Langtry, the first of many stars of the theatre. Dame Ellen Terry, Sir George Robey, Sir John Gielgud, Dame Margot Fonteyn and Sir Robert Helpmann have all played here.

The unprepossessing exterior of the church at Deerhurst conceals a Saxon gem

dedicated, in part, to the life of the composer and partly to an evocation of life in Regency and Victorian Cheltenham. Holst was a pupil at the Grammar School and at the age of 17 had already heard his *Scherzo* performed at the Montpellier Rotunda.

There are a number of villages in the vicinity of Cheltenham worth visiting. Many are mentioned under their own heading but, among those that are not, Prestbury, home of the racecourse and practically part of Cheltenham, must not be overlooked as it claims to be the most haunted village in Britain. Syde and Brimpsfield, 5 miles (8km) to the south of Cheltenham, are noted for their interesting churches; and Miserden, an estate village of some charm is close to Misarden Park, an Elizabethan mansion set in lovely gardens which are open to the public.

DEERHURST AND ODDA'S CHAPEL Gloucestershire
Map ref SO8730

An attractive vale farming village of cottages in a variety of styles, with some fine examples of cruck-construction timber-framed houses, Deerhurst is splendidly located on the wide, grassy east bank of the Severn. Now a small village, a thousand years ago it was the site of the chief monastery of the Hwicce, the Anglo-Saxon people that ruled the kingdom of the lower Severn. It has two claims to fame: a largely Saxon parish church and an almost complete Saxon chapel.

The church, St Mary's Priory, was once part of an important monastery founded in the late 8th century by the Hwicce. An early Archbishop of Canterbury, St Aelfheah (Alphege), was a monk here. Such was its importance that the Danish King Canute signed a treaty here with Edmund Ironside in 1016. The church is the only remaining Saxon monastic church in the country and there still remain several Saxon doors and windows and a 9th-century font (the finest in England), as well as a number of medieval and later features. Particularly striking is the double-headed window high up on the

A replica of the Odda Stone, set into the wall of this remarkable chapel, tells the story of its construction

west wall which is possibly made up of old Roman stones; the animal-headed label stops (the carved ends of dripstones) in the middle doorway below date from the early 9th century. The Deerhurst Angel is the name given to a carving, also of the 9th century, on the surviving arch of the Saxon apse, now on the east exterior. Of the features from later centuries the most interesting are those pews which, in Puritan fashion, surround the communion table.

A mere 200 yards (183m) southwest of the church, beyond a converted barn, is a stone building seemingly tacked on to a handsome half-timbered Tudor farmhouse. This is Odda's Chapel, once concealed behind walls added throughout later centuries and only revealed as a complete Saxon chapel in 1885. The discovery in 1675 of an inscribed tablet in a local orchard dates its construction precisely to 1056 when Earl Odda, a kinsman of Edward the Confessor, built it as part of a royal hall in memory of his brother Aelfric who had died at Deerhurst three years before. At the time of its discovery the chancel had been divided with floors whilst the nave had become a kitchen.

THE 'LOST' SAXON CHAPEL

The discovery of Odda's Chapel was one of the great architectural finds of the 19th century. As repairs were being carried out on the neighbouring farmhouse, Abbots Court, traces of a semi-circular arch came to light and the further removal of plasterwork revealed a complete Saxon chapel. The Odda Stone that had already been discovered near by led experts to conclude that this was the chapel mentioned on it. A copy of the stone, inscribed in Latin, is placed on the wall inside. For those whose Latin is rusty the translation is: 'Earl Odda ordered this royal hall to be built and dedicated in honour of the Holy Trinity for the soul of his brother Aelfric which left his body in this place. Aldred, Bishop of Worcester, dedicated it on the 2nd of the Ides of April in the 14th year of King Edward, King of the English'.

A River and a Saxon Chapel

Just beneath the Cotswold escarpment flows Britain's longest river, the Severn. Part of this walk, perfect in late spring or summer, takes you along the riverbank and visits a complete Saxon chapel. Good level walking along field paths, which can be muddy.

Time: 2 hours. Distance: 3½ miles (5.6km).
Location: 5 miles (8km) southwest of Tewkesbury.
Start: Apperley village hall, a quarter of a mile (400m) off the B4213 between the A38 and A417. (OS grid ref: SO866285.)
OS Map: Explorer 179 (Cheltenham, Gloucester & Stroud) 1:25,000.
See Key to Walks on page 121.

ROUTE DIRECTIONS

From the hall in **Apperley** walk across the grass to a stile, then proceed to a small bridge and stile into a field. Head straight across the field on a defined path to climb a further stile, then follow a clear, grassy path with a young sapling wood to your left. Keep to the path as it curves right eventually reaching a stile flanking a gate in the field corner. At the lane beyond, turn immediately right through a metal gate into another field, and bear left across the corner for 30 yards (27m) to a stile, well hidden in the hedge.

From the top of the large sloping meadow beyond, head downhill, soon crossing another stile, pass to the right of a modern house and climb a stile into the adjoining part of the meadow. Bear diagonally left in the direction of a thatched cottage, then look out for a stile in the hedge to your left and drop down on to a narrow lane.

Turn right, pass a gate to your right, then shortly mount an odd concrete platform on the left by a house.

Keep straight ahead along a bank on the left-hand margin of the garden to a stile and enter a wide meadow, formerly the site of **Deerhurst** Abbey. Head across the field, bearing slightly right towards a half-timbered building abutted by a stone building – **Odda's Chapel**. Pass over a stile located beside them and follow a track for 100 yards (91m) until you reach the **River Severn**. Turn left along the riverbank and remain on this scenic path which passes through a series of gates and across stiles. The path eventually leaves the meadows behind, becoming more enclosed, and then narrows further as you pass behind a house.

Continue across a meadow and climb a stile into the car park of the Coal House Inn. Pass in front of the pub and turn left to follow a lane that curves behind the pub. Almost immediately, turn right along a track, cross a

Half-timbering and an attractive garden at Apperley

cattle grid and look out for a stile across the grass slightly to your right. Follow the path, which runs almost in a straight line, across sloping meadows and stiles to reach a level field, then pass to the left of a farm and stables to a gate and the lane in Apperley. Turn left, pass the post office, then turn right back to the village hall.

POINTS OF INTEREST

Apperley
A scattered village very typical of the Severn Vale, with some particularly fine examples of half-timbered buildings, including the village post office.

Deerhurst
This rather dispersed riverside village is particularly noted for its Saxon connections. Edmund Ironside signed a treaty here with King Canute in 1016, whilst the parish church, St Mary's Priory, is the only Anglo-Saxon monastic

church surviving in England. Inside, there is a fine Saxon font and window. The so-called Deerhurst Angel, a 9th-century carving, can be found on the arch of an exterior apse.

Odda's Chapel
Situated near the priory church is Odda's Chapel, one of the only complete Saxon chapels in the

country. Earl Odda, ally of Edward the Confessor, was a Saxon aristocrat who ruled much of southwest England, and according to the tablet found in a nearby orchard in 1675, he built the chapel in 1056. The chapel was only discovered in 1885.

River Severn
Once an important commercial waterway for the Midlands and linked to the Thames by the Thames and Severn Canal, the Severn is the longest river in Britain. Now it is chiefly used by pleasure craft and much visited at certain times of year for the Severn Bore, a tidal wave that can sometimes reach 9 feet (2.75m) in height.

Pocked by age and the weather, a gargoyle stares down from St Mary's Priory, Deerhurst

The delightful stylised memorial to Thomas and Christian Machen in Gloucester Cathedral portrays the entire family

GLOUCESTER'S COMPOSERS

The Cotswolds seem to have produced more than their fair share of composers and the vale, and Gloucester in particular, is not to be outdone in this respect. John Stafford Smith was born in 1750, and studied music in London. He became an organist at the Chapel Royal and wrote a song for the Anachreontic Society, a select group of artists and *bon viveurs*, well known on both sides of the Atlantic. In 1812 a British attack on a Baltimore fort led an American prisoner to write some lines to Stafford Smith's tune – this became *The Star Spangled Banner*, now the national anthem of the United States.

Ivor Gurney was born in Queen Street in 1890. He was a chorister at the cathedral school and later began to produce musical settings to the poetry of Bridges and Housman. During World War I he took to writing verse in the trenches to critical acclaim. It seems that the war exacerbated his already fragile mental state and although he continued to write and compose after the war, under the tutelage of Vaughan Williams, a suicide attempt led to committal to an asylum. He died of tuberculosis in 1937 and is buried at Twigworth.

GLOUCESTER Gloucestershire Map ref SO8318

For a town of such immense historical importance, Gloucester has suffered aesthetically. There is, in fact, quite a lot to see, but with the obvious exception of the cathedral, it has to be sought out.

For many centuries, Gloucester was one of the most important cities in the kingdom. It was founded as Roman *Glevum*, at first as a garrison town on the western edge of occupied England and then as a 'colonia', populated by retired legionnaires who were rewarded with a villa and a sinecure. Under the Saxons it regained importance in the 7th century when the monastery of St Peter was established; the modern street plan is closer to the Saxon rather than the Roman town. Once it had become the capital of a Saxon shire, Edward the Confessor held his winter court here, a tradition continued by William I who announced in Gloucester his great undertaking, the Domesday Book. Soon after, work started on the abbey church that was to become the city's landmark, its Cathedral of St Peter. In 1216 Henry III was crowned in Gloucester (the only monarch to have been crowned outside Westminster) and in 1327 the murdered Edward II was buried here, a fact that subsequently turned Gloucester into a place of pilgrimage until the Dissolution of the Monasteries.

Gloucester became an important Severn port during the reign of Elizabeth I. The city had Parliamentarian sympathies during the Civil War and withstood the long siege by the Royalists; subsequently Charles II destroyed the walls and withdrew many privileges. The docks finally went into decline in the 19th century with the advent of larger ships.

The points of interest are scattered throughout the city and an early visit is recommended to the Tourist Information Centre, located in St Michael's Tower at The Cross, site of the ancient 13th-century stone cross removed in 1751 'for the better conveniency of carriages', and meeting point of Gloucester's four principal streets – Westgate, Eastgate, Southgate and Northgate. Inevitably, the cathedral remains the focal point of the city, a veritable pearl in a gritty oyster shell.

Gloucester Cathedral is situated just to the north of The Cross, its monumental tower visible from afar. Built on the site of a Saxon abbey, it was William I who appointed Serlo, a Benedictine monk from Mont St Michel, as abbot. Serlo resuscitated the ailing abbey and began its reconstruction during the reign of William Rufus. It was consecrated in 1100 and completed in 1120, although additions were made over the following centuries. At the Dissolution of the Monasteries, the Abbey Church of St Peter was rededicated to the Holy and Invisible Trinity, becoming the cathedral church of the new diocese of Gloucester. It is an outstanding example of medieval ecclesiastical architecture, a successful blend of Norman and Perpendicular.

The tower, dating from 1450, replaces the earlier smaller tower and spire and contains Great Peter, the last medieval Bourdon bell. The nave is lined with magnificent Norman arcading, its vault dating back to 1242 together with the roof which was constructed from 110 oak trees from the Forest of Dean. The South Transept is a very early example of the Perpendicular style, whilst the Norman crypt reflects the original Norman church above. See, too, the massive east window of 1349, the beautifully carved 14th-century choirstalls, the Lady Chapel in late Perpendicular style, the tomb of Edward II and the Norman chapter house.

The Cathedral Green is surrounded by a fine array of houses from the 16th, 17th and 18th centuries, as well as the 15th-century half-timbered Parliament Room, where Richard II held Parliament in 1378. In College Court, just off College Green, is the House of the Tailor of Gloucester, the shop where the story by Beatrix Potter was set and which is now a shop and museum.

GEORGE WHITFIELD
An important character associated with Gloucester was George Whitfield, one of the earliest Methodists. Born in 1714, the youngest of seven children, he was educated at Oxford where he met Charles and John Wesley and joined their religious group. His devotion to fasting and praying outdoors in all weathers affected his health and he returned to Gloucester to become a deacon. However, the Church of England disapproved of his links with Dissenters and he took to touring England and America with a portable pulpit. Whitfield had a remarkable oratorical style and a voice which, so Benjamin Franklin said, 'could be heard by 30,000 people at one time'. More than 50 colleges and schools in America owe their existence to him.

The soaring roof of the cathedral

Gloucester's historic dockland has been fashionably revitalised

THE GLOUCESTER & SHARPNESS CANAL

Originally it was hoped to build a canal from Berkeley Pill to Gloucester in order to avoid the difficult Severn route but it was only in 1827 that a shorter version from Sharpness, where the Old Dock was linked by a lock to the Severn, saw the light of day. The New Dock, still used, was built in 1874. Near by is a large stone pier, all that remains of the 1879 Severn Railway Bridge which was demolished in 1969 after being struck by a ship. The canal banks are dotted with a number of charming bridge-keepers' cottages decorated with Doric columns.

Whilst the docks themselves are long since redundant, a walk around them is worthwhile for the residual atmosphere of Victorian commerce. Many of the warehouses have been resurrected as offices, restaurants and museums, among them the Robert Opie Collection at the Museum of Advertising and Packaging, and the National Waterways Museum, both exceptionally interesting. In another warehouse is the Gloucester Antiques Centre, containing some 60 shops. At the north end of the docks is the Old Customs House which now houses the Regiments of Gloucestershire Museum.

A walk through the bustle of the city's main streets is recommended. The medieval New Inn, a short way from The Cross along Northgate Street, designed to accommodate the growing number of visitors to the tomb of Edward II in the 15th century, is built around a beautiful galleried courtyard. On Southgate Street, the Church of St Mary de Crypt is a fine example of the Perpendicular style, although in its history its crypt has been a tavern and the whole church became an explosives factory during the Siege of Gloucester in 1643.

The remains of the Roman Wall can be viewed on King's Walk, just off Eastgate Street, whilst Blackfriars is the finest surviving Dominican Friary in the country, but awaits restoration. For aficionados of museums there are several others worth seeing – Gloucester Museum and Art Gallery on Brunswick Road contains Roman mosaics and the Birdlip Mirror, together with a Natural History section with a freshwater aquarium, and an excellent art collection. The Folk Museum is housed in some fine half-timbered houses on Westgate Street, whilst the Transport Museum is on Bearland, in an old fire station. Not far from here is Ladybellgate House, the finest town house in Gloucester. Recently the first Prison Museum attached to an operational prison has opened, explaining its history from 1792 to the present day.

A few miles to the south of Gloucester on a Cotswold outlier, 651 feet (198m) high, is the Robinswood Hill Country Park. The old quarry on its west side is a Site of Special Scientific Interest because of its exposure of lower and middle lias rock, the finest inland example in the country.

SLIMBRIDGE Gloucestershire Map ref SO7303
The Wildfowl and Wetlands Trust at Slimbridge is the inspiration of the late Sir Peter Scott, artist and naturalist. Established as the Severn Wildfowl Trust in 1946, the saltmarshes around the Gloucester and Sharpness Canal and the River Severn have now become the home of the greatest collection of waterfowl in the world, from swans and geese to flamingos and humming birds. Excellent viewing facilities are available and, in winter, towers and hides provide remarkable views of migrating birds.

The village itself, which, like North Nibley, is the possible birthplace of William Tyndale, translator of the Bible from Latin into English, is certainly well worth a visit. It also boasts a 13th-century church, a very fine example of Early English style. Behind the church is the Rectory, which stands on the site of the early Manor House from where Maurice of Berkeley, a scion of the great Berkeley dynasty, left to fight at the Battle of Bannockburn in 1314.

Two miles (3.2km) north of Slimbridge is Frampton-on-Severn, an extensive village which is said to have the largest green in England. The restored church contains a rare lead Norman font.

HUMPTY DUMPTY
The origin of the nursery rhyme Humpty Dumpty can be traced back to the Siege of Gloucester of 1643. The subject refers to Royalist siege-engines which fell over and were rendered useless by the mud of the city ditch.

WINTER VISITORS
Slimbridge is the winter home of Bewick's swans, which migrate every year from Siberia, and whooper swans which come mainly from Iceland. They pair for life and some pairs have been coming to Slimbridge for over 20 years. The Trust operates an adoption scheme to help ensure their future.

The many hundreds of swans which pass through Slimbridge are recognised by their bill and facial markings

ANCIENT INNS

Tewkesbury has a number of old and interesting inns. The Hop Pole in Church Street was featured in *Pickwick Papers*, the novel by Charles Dickens; the Tudor House in the High Street was built in 1540, the Old Black Bear near the junction with Mythe Road possibly dates back to 1308, whilst the Ancient Grudge takes its name from the Wars of the Roses.

TEWKESBURY Gloucestershire Map ref SO8932

Tewkesbury's considerable historical significance was largely governed by its location on the banks of the rivers Severn and Avon which were instrumental in the 16th-century cloth and mustard trade and the later flour trade. Its importance depended, too, on its medieval Benedictine monastery of which only the magnificent church remains. This was built by the Norman, Robert Fitzhamon, who used the Severn to import stone from Normandy for its construction. After his death the 'Honour of Tewkesbury', as the patronage came to be known, passed to an illegitimate son of Henry I and then to the de Clare family. The abbey became one of the most powerful in the kingdom, owning large areas of sheep grazing land and building many fine tithe barns in the process – some of these survive, for example at Stanway. In 1539 the abbey was dissolved but Tewkesbury's citizens bought the church for the total sum of £483.

Because of its location close to two rivers which, even now, tend to flood, and with the abbey lands at its back, the town, unable to expand, folded in on itself. Throughout the 17th and 18th centuries this was achieved by building around narrow alleyways, several of which have survived (Machine Court, Fish Alley, Fryzier Alley) off the main streets – Barton Street, Church Street and High Street. There is, therefore, a great deal more of Tewkesbury than is at first evident to the eye, although its collection of half-timbered and brick houses presents one of the finest historical ensembles in the country.

However, the town is dominated by the Abbey Church of St Mary and the eye filled by its great 132-foot (41m) square tower. Inside one of the most striking features is the set of 14 Norman pillars which support the 14th-century roof. The choir is illuminated by 14th-century stained-glass windows, whilst around it radiate six chapels containing monuments to the wealthy families

The massive bulk of Tewkesbury Abbey once lay at the centre of a powerful monastic empire

that have influenced both the church and the town. The west front exterior is notable for its Norman arch, of almost unsurpassed grandeur.

There is a lot to enjoy in the town, all accessible on foot. A circular walk includes, in the dry season, a stroll across the Ham – a huge meadow that separates the Mill Avon from the Severn and which invariably floods each winter – to the river.

Opposite the church is the handsome Bell Hotel. From here Mill Street leads you down to Abel Fletcher's Mill, so called because it is thought to have played a role in the Victorian novel, *John Halifax, Gentleman*, much of which is set in the imaginary town of Nortonbury, which was modelled on Tewkesbury. From here you can either walk along St Mary's Road, with its attractive timbered cottages, or cross the Avon and strike out across the Ham. Owned by the town, the grass of the Ham is cut each year and auctioned following a centuries-old tradition.

At the Severn turn right to walk along by the weir and then return across the meadow this side of the flour mills. You can cross the old mill bridge and then walk along the Avon. At King John's Bridge recross the river and turn right into the High Street to the The Cross, now a memorial but the site of the medieval High Cross razed by Puritans in 1650.

On your left Barton Street will take you to Tewkesbury Museum in a 17th-century building that also houses the Tourist Information Centre. The museum features a model of the Battle of Tewkesbury. Church Street, to your right, takes you past the distinctive Hop Pole Hotel which featured in Charles Dickens' novel *Pickwick Papers*. Beyond this is a row of restored 15th-century cottages

A patchwork of half-timbered cottages on St Mary's Road

LITERARY ASSOCIATIONS
Tewkesbury has several literary associations as we have seen. There are others; Barbara Cartland (1901–2000) had links with the town and the family monument is to be found in the churchyard. The organ within the abbey church was played by the poet John Milton when it was located at Hampton Court. Daniel Defoe's observations on the town are recorded in his *Tour through the Whole Island of Great Britain*, published in 1724–26. He called Tewkesbury 'a large and very populous town situated upon the River Avon' famous 'for a great manufacture of stockings'. Seventy years later the essayist William Hazlitt, walking from Shropshire to Somerset, spent the night in a Tewkesbury inn reading Saint Pierre's *Paul and Virginia*.

After the Battle of Tewkesbury in 1417, perhaps the most decisive battle of the Wars of the Roses, many of the defeated Lancastrian troops sought sanctuary in the church but were slain nonetheless. 'Bloody Meadow' as the battlefield came to be known, is south of the church, off Lincoln Green Lane, and there is a 'Battlefield Trail' to follow.

built by medieval merchants. One, known as the Merchant's Cottage or the Little Museum, is presented in much the way it would have looked in its heyday. Another, the John Moore Countryside Museum, takes its name from the local writer whose stories were based on Tewkesbury and the countryside and villages around nearby Bredon.

On the right, an alleyway leads down to the Baptist Chapel. Although the building dates back to the 15th century, it became a chapel only in the 17th century.

THORNBURY Gloucestershire Map ref ST6390
An attractive market town just north of Bristol in the county of Gloucestershire, Thornbury is well known for its Tudor castle, built in 1510 by Edward Stafford, 3rd Duke of Buckingham, Constable of England. Thornbury Castle was later appropriated by Henry VIII and he stayed here with Anne Boleyn in 1535. Mary Tudor returned the castle to the Staffords but after the Civil War it fell to ruin until 1824 when it became the residence of the Howard family. Now a luxury hotel, it is particularly noted for the handsome brick double chimney and the fine tracery of its oriel windows.

The Church of St Mary the Virgin has a fine medieval tower which apparently sways a full six inches when the peal of eight bells is rung. Inside there is an unusual medieval stone pulpit. A cottage on Chapel Street now houses Thornbury Museum.

Hanging baskets and pretty, pastel-washed shops add colour to Thornbury town centre

The Severn Vale and the Vale of Berkeley

Leisure Information
Places of Interest
Shopping
The Performing Arts
Sports, Activities and the
Outdoors
Annual Events and Customs

Checklist

Leisure Information

TOURIST INFORMATION OFFICES

Cheltenham
Cheltenham Municipal Offices, 77 The Promenade. Tel: 01242 522878.
www.visitcheltenham.gov.uk
Gloucester
28 Southgate Street. Tel: 01452 421188.
A local information service is available at Gloucester Docks in the National Waterways Museum. Tel: 01452 318061.
Tewkesbury
The Museum, 64 Barton Street. Tel: 01684 295027.
www.tewkesburybc.gov.uk
Thornbury
The Town Hall, Old Police Station, High Street. Tel: 01454 281638.

OTHER INFORMATION

English Heritage
29 Queen Square, Bristol. Tel: 0117 975 0700
www.english-heritage.org.uk
National Trust
Severn Region, Mythe End House, Tewkesbury. Tel: 01684 850051.
www.nationaltrust.org.uk

Parking
In small towns and villages please park with care avoiding driveways and entrances to fields and leave sufficient space for lorries and tractors to pass.

ORDNANCE SURVEY MAPS

Landranger 1:50,000 Sheets 150, 162, 172.

Places of Interest

There will be an admission charge at the following places of interest unless otherwise stated.

Berkeley Castle
Tel: 01453 810332. Also Butterfly farm. Open Apr–Oct, most days.
Blackfriars Dominican Friary
Ladybellgate, Gloucester. Tel: 0117 9750700. Open Apr–Sep, most days. Free.
Cheltenham Art Gallery and Museum
Clarence Street, Cheltenham.

Hundreds of beautiful butterflies fly free in the specially built butterfly house at Berkeley Castle

Tel: 01242 237431. Permanent and temporary exhibitions. Open all year, most days. Free.

Cheltenham Racecourse Hall of Fame
The Racecourse, Prestbury Park, Cheltenham. Tel: 01242 513014. The story of steeple chasing at Cheltenham. Open all year, daily. Free.

City Museum and Art Gallery
Brunswick Road, Gloucester. Tel: 01452 524131. Open all year, most days. Free.

Dinosaur Valley
The Docks, Gloucester. Tel: 01452 311265. Open all year, most days; daily during summer holidays.

Gloucester Folk Museum
99–103 Westgate Street, Gloucester. Tel: 01452 526467. Tudor and Jacobean houses showing folklore, crafts and social history of Gloucestershire. Open all year, most days. Free.

Holst Birthplace Museum
4 Clarence Road, Pittville, Cheltenham. Tel: 01242 524846. Home and birthplace of Gustav Holst who was born in this Regency house in 1874. The rooms have been carefully restored in the tradition of 'upstairs, downstairs'. Open all year, most days.

House of the Tailor of Gloucester
College Court, Gloucester. Tel: 01452 422856. Small gift shop and exhibition devoted to Beatrix Potter. Open most days.

Jenner Museum
Church Lane, High Street, Berkeley. Tel: 01453 810631. Shows Jenner's life as an 18th-century doctor. Open Apr–Sep, daily; closed Mon, except Bank Holidays; Oct, Sun afternoons only.

Misarden Park Gardens
Miserden. Tel: 01285 821303. Beautiful gardens surrounding Elizabethan mansion. Open Apr–Sep, on certain days.

John Moore Countryside Museum
41 Church Street, Tewkesbury. Tel: 01684 297174. Open Apr–Oct, most days.

National Waterways Museum
Llanthony Warehouse, Gloucester Docks, Gloucester. Tel: 01452 318054. Displays cover 200 years of the history of inland waterways. Re-creation of a traditional canal maintenance yard, demonstrations, boats to visit. Open all year, daily.

Nature in Art
Wallsworth Hall, Tewkesbury Road, Twigworth, Gloucester. Tel: 01452 731422. Museum dedicated to art inspired by nature. Demonstrations Feb–Oct. Open all year, most days.

Odda's Chapel
Off B4213 near River Severn, Deerhurst. Open all year. Free.

Old Baptist Chapel
Old Baptist Chapel Court, Tewkesbury. Tel: 01684 299893. Open all year, daily. Free.

Oldbury Power Station
Oldbury. Tel: 01454 419899. Guided tours last an hour and a half. Also nature trail and a visitor centre. Open Mar–Oct, daily, or by appointment. Free.

Pittville Pump Room and Museum
Pittville Park, Cheltenham. Tel: 01242 523852. Open all year, most days. Free admission to Pump Room. Closed Tuesdays.

The Prison Museum
Barrack Square, Gloucester. Tel: 01452 529551. Open Apr–Sep, most days.

Robert Opie Collection – Museum of Advertising and Packaging
Albert Warehouse, Gloucester Docks, Gloucester. Tel: 01452 302309. Story of labels and items that crowd childhood memories. Open: summer, daily; winter: most days.

Soldiers of Gloucestershire Museum
Custom House, The Docks, Gloucester. Tel: 01452 522682. Story of Gloucestershire's soldiers in peace and war. Open all year, most days; Jun–Sep, open daily.

Tewkesbury Town Museum
64 Barton Street, Tewkesbury. Tel: 01684 295027. Open Easter–Oct, daily.

Wildfowl and Wetlands Trust
Slimbridge.Tel: 01453 890333. Watch the migrating wildfowl from hides and viewing towers. Educational exhibition and tropical house. Open all year, daily.

SPECIAL INTEREST FOR CHILDREN

The following places may be of interest to visitors with children. Unless otherwise stated, there will be an admission charge.

St Augustine's Farm
Arlingham, Gloucester. Tel: 01452 740277. Working farm close to the river. Visitors may feed some animals. Picnic and play area. Open all year, most days.

Old Down House
Oldown, Tockington, Bristol. Tel: 01454 413605. Victorian kitchen and garden, farm, adventure walks and animals. Open all year, daily.

Wildfowl and Wetlands Trust
Slimbridge. Tel: 01453 890333. Hides, viewing towers, permanent educational exhibition, Tropical House. Open all year, daily.

Shopping

Cheltenham
A Farmers' Market is held on the Promendade on the last Friday of each month.
The main shopping areas are: High Street, the Promenade, Montpellier, Regent Street. For antiques and crafts shops: Montpellier Terrace and Norwood Road.

Gloucester
Market, Wed.
The main shopping areas are in the four main streets that converge at The Cross. In the Eastgate area there are two covered shopping malls – King's Walks and Market Way. The Gloucester Antiques Centre, Severn Road, The Docks has over 60 antiques shops under one roof.

Tewkesbury
Market, Sat.

LOCAL SPECIALITIES

Cider is produced in the area, look for signs outside farms.

The Performing Arts

Everyman Theatre
Regent Street, Cheltenham. Tel: 01242 572573.
Guildhall Arts Centre
23 Eastgate Street, Gloucester. Tel: 01452 505086. An arts centre with films, workshops, events and exhibitions.
Kings Theatre
Gloucester. Tel: 01452 300130.
New Olympus Theatre
Gloucester. Tel: 01452 525917.
Playhouse Theatre
49 Bath Road, Cheltenham. Tel: 01242 522852.
Roses Theatre
Tewkesbury. Tel: 01684 295074.
Sub Tone
117 Promenade. Tel: 01242 575925. Jazz club.

Sports, Activities and the Outdoors

ANGLING

Coarse
Tewkesbury
Permits can be obtained from: The Fishing Tackle Shop in Tewkesbury, Tel: 01684 293234. Witcombe Waters, Tel: 01452 863591.

BOAT HIRE

Tewkesbury
Telstar Cruises Ltd. Tel: 01684 294088.

BOAT TRIPS

Severn Leisure Cruises operate from Upton-on-Severn. Tel: 01684 593112.

CRICKET

Cheltenham
Cheltenham College Grounds, Thirlestaine Road.
Gloucester
King's School Grounds, St Oswald's Road.

CYCLING

Cheltenham
Crabtrees, 50 Winchcombe Street. Tel: 01242 515291.

GOLF COURSES

Gloucester
Gloucester Hotel and Country Club, Matson Lane, Robinswood Hill. Tel: 01452 411331.
Tewkesbury
Tewkesbury Park Hotel Golf and Country Club, Lincoln Green Lane. Tel: 01684 295405.

GUIDED WALKS

Cotswolds Walking Holidays Ltd, 10 Royal Parade, Bayshill Road, Cheltenham. Tel: 01242 254353, Fax: 01242 51888. Organised walking holidays in the area, weekend breaks and village to village walks.
The Voluntary Wardens, a volunteer arm of the Countryside Service, arrange guided walks. Tel: 01452 425674.

HORSE RACING

Cheltenham
Cheltenham Racecourse, Prestbury Park, Cheltenham. Tel: 01242 513014.

HORSE-RIDING

Brookthorpe
Cotswold Trail Riding, Ongers Farm, Upton Lane. Tel: 01452 813344.
Hardwicke
Summer House Equitation Centre. Tel: 01452 720288

PARAGLIDING

Cheltenham
The Flight Factory, Prestbury Park. Tel: 01242 261621.

SKIING

Robinswood Hill
Robinswood Hill Dry Ski Slope. Tel: 01452 414300.

Annual Events and Customs

Cheltenham
Folk Festival, February.
National Hunt Festival including the Gold Cup, Prestbury Park. March.
Jazz Festival, April.
Cheltenham Cricket Festival, usually held in July.
International Festival of Music, July.
Festival of Literature, October.
Cheltenham Pittville on Sunday. Pittville Park. Every Sunday from late May to late September. Live music, brunches and teas.
Gloucester
Gloucester Cricket Festival, usually held in May.
Three Choirs Festival, Europe's oldest choir festival is held alternately in Gloucester, Hereford and Worcester.
Tewkesbury
Medieval Fair, July.

A summer game of cricket has room to spare at Frampton-on-Severn, which claims the largest village green in England

The Southern Cotswolds

The southern Cotswolds are different in character from the northern part – if the north is golden, the south is silver. In the south (here we mean south of a line drawn approximately between Painswick and Northleach) the escarpment is lower, but the valleys are steeper; the dappled stone is heavier seeming, in keeping with its industrial heritage. The medieval wool industry moved from the high wolds to these steeper valleys to make use of the fast-flowing streams, above all in the Stroud Valley. Pretty villages abound, particularly along the Coln Valley whilst the Roman Cotswolds are embodied in Cirencester, Chedworth and Bath.

BATH Somerset Map ref ST7464

One of the most magnificent towns in Europe, Bath is known chiefly for its Roman baths (hence the name) and for the elegance of its Georgian architecture, the result of its fashionable re-emergence as a spa in the 18th century. Although not strictly speaking a Cotswold town, Bath is nonetheless somehow inseparable from the area, not least because the aspect that gives it character, its buildings, are made of Cotswold limestone.

The open square in front of the abbey is a popular venue during Bath's summer music festival

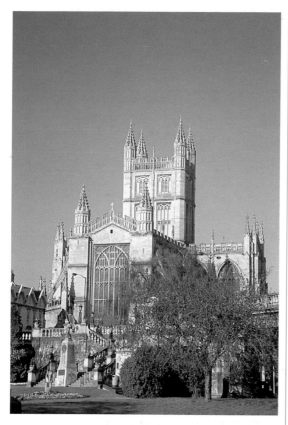

The tall abbey tower is a good landmark for getting your bearings in the city

THE ROYAL SWINEHERD
According to legend Bath was founded some 2,800 years ago, by Prince Bladud, father of King Lear and a Trojan refugee. The Prince, a leper, was banished to the salt marshes of the area to herd pigs. One of his pigs caught the disease but recovered after bathing in the hot springs. Bladud cured himself in the same way and, thus, the city was born.

THE GOOD AND THE GREAT
Naturally, Bath has played host to a large number among the good and great. Sir Walter Scott stayed at what is now Pratt's Hotel, Shelley at 5 Abbey Church Yard, Dickens at the Saracen's Head (Moses Pickwick, the inspiration for his great character, resided in Great Pulteney Street), and, in their time, both Lord Nelson and Handel lived in Pierrepont Street. Lord Robert Clive, or 'Clive of India', resided at the Circus, as did the painter Thomas Gainsborough. Robert Southey, Poet Laureate from 1813 to 1843, lived at Walcot Street. In Kingsmead the playwright Richard Sheridan lived at New King Street and in the Bathwick and Widcombe area Jane Austen lived, for a time, in Sydney Place.

Archaeological evidence indicates that the first settlement, *Aquae Sulis*, was Roman. After a hiatus following the departure of the Romans, an important Saxon abbey was built here, and then a Norman cathedral. The waters continued to be used, but it was not until the 17th century, when the wool trade began its decline, that the fashion for using medicinal waters induced a new construction under the aegis of Master of Ceremonies, Richard 'Beau' Nash, architect John Wood and, later, City Surveyor, Thomas Baldwin.

The town is dramatically draped over the surrounding hills, presenting a magnificent aspect which can be viewed from many of the streets on the upper slopes. There is a great deal to see in Bath but many of the highlights can be enjoyed on foot, and since parking can be a problem, use the park-and-ride system. The bus from the Lansdown car park sets you down at Queen's Square, which is a good place to start walking.

The centre of Bath can be divided into four – the oldest part is the city centre around the abbey and baths; the Upper Town was built as the town expanded, whilst Kingsmead, now the liveliest area at night, used to house

Bath's formal architecture is offset by a number of pleasant parks, including the floral Parade Gardens

PLEASANT PARKS

Bath is a city of parks. Royal Victoria Park, beneath Royal Crescent, was originally laid out to be an arboretum in 1829 and at its far western end are the Botanical Gardens which specialise in plants that flourish in limestone soils. Also here is the Georgian Garden, recreated to show how a Bath garden would have looked in the late 18th century. Right in the centre of Bath are Parade Gardens, famous for their flower displays, whilst concerts are given from the bandstand in the summer.

THE BATH SPA PROJECT

The Bath Spa Project, due to be completed in summer 2002, will provide the city with the only working traditional spa in the UK. The historic Cross Bath and the Hot (or Old Royal) Bath are undergoing restoration and will re-open alongside the new spa building which will house the main spa complex.

the sick and poor. Bathwick and Widcombe are west of the Pulteney Bridge. The following walk through the city takes in part of the first three areas; places not featured are described after.

Queen Square was John Wood's first important work and takes its name from Queen Caroline, consort of George II. The obelisk in the centre was built to honour the visit of the Prince and Princess of Wales in 1738. Wood's masterpiece, the Circus, begun in 1754, is at the top of Gay Street, which runs north from Queen Square. It is a design of great originality, the façade of each of the three floors is framed in a series of columns, from bottom to top, Doric, Ionic and Corinthian.

From here it is but a short stroll west along Brock Street to another magnificent ensemble, the Royal Crescent, begun by John Wood's son in 1767. Number 1, open to the public, has been restored to look as it would have done some 200 years ago. A longer walk would take you further north to a number of other crescents, those of Camden, Cavendish, Lansdown and Somerset Place. Behind Lansdown Crescent is Beckford's Walk, replete with the follies placed there by the eccentric millionaire William Beckford.

Gravel Walk, opposite No 1 Royal Crescent, threads through parkland to Queen's Parade Place. Turn left, then left again to re-enter Gay Street and then turn right into George Street and right again into Milsom Street. Continue into Burton Street as it becomes Union Street and turn left into Northumberland Place. Pass through this little alley of shops to the High Street and cross over to the Guildhall. This was designed in 1776 by Thomas Baldwin and includes a sumptuous banqueting room, in Adam style, which is adorned with elegant 18th-century crystal chandeliers.

Beyond the Guildhall is the covered market. On the other side is Grand Parade and the River Avon and to the left the magnificence of Pulteney Bridge, designed by Robert Adam in 1769 and one of only very few bridges in the world that is lined by shops on both sides. On the other side of the bridge is a marvellous vista down Great Pulteney Street towards the Holburne Museum and also the steps down to the riverside walk.

Turning right along Grand Parade will bring you to Orange Grove. Pass the east end of the abbey and continue down Terrace Walk. By the Huntsman Inn, turn right down North Parade Passage to Sally Lunn's House, built in 1622 and one of the oldest houses in Bath. Here Sally Lunn created her famous Bath buns and the original faggot oven and period kitchenware are still exhibited. Although it is still a coffee house, it is also a museum and the medieval and Roman excavations are the largest on show in Bath.

North Parade Passage emerges at Abbey Green. Turn right here for the abbey itself, the third to be built on this site. The first was built in the 8th century by Offa, King of Mercia, and Edgar, the first king of a united England was crowned here in AD 973. The Norman abbey, built in the 12th century, fell into disrepair and was replaced by this smaller version. Inside, after passing a manned desk where 'voluntary' payment is expected, there is much to admire – its magnificent ceiling and windows, and array of plaques, some of which make fascinating reading. The Heritage Vaults tell the story of the abbey and include Saxon and Norman stonework and a reconstruction of the Norman cathedral.

In the courtyard outside, a favourite place with buskers and performers in general, the National Trust shop is in Marshall Wade's House, the oldest Palladian style building in Bath. Opposite are the Roman baths

CITY OF CULTURE

Bath has an old and thriving theatre and the city plays host to an increasing number of festivals. Most famous is the festival, in June, of mainly 18th-century music. Founded in 1948, it was revived in 1959, helped by the involvement of Sir Yehudi Menuhin. Nowadays the festival includes modern compositions, art exhibitions and poetry. The Mozartfest is held in November and the Literature Festival takes place in February and March. Casual entertainment is found on the pavements around the Abbey where a grand variety of buskers regularly perform.

Like fine Pulteney Street, the famous Pulteney Bridge was named after one of the city's great 18th-century improvers, William Pulteney

CYCLE ROUTE
Bath has a leisure route for cyclists, the Avon Cycleway, which follows the disused railway line through the city along the course of the Avon river valley. Maps of the route are available from the Tourist Information Centre. On Sundays organised rides, along the cycleway and elsewhere, depart from Bath Spa Station with the Cyclists Touring Club.

Royal Crescent offers a vista of breathtaking symmetry, and a glimpse of gracious living at No 1

themselves, a well-preserved area of ancient pools and saunas where something of that era still lingers. The remains of a temple can be seen here, as well as a number of items discovered in the area of the baths (which used to extend beneath the Pump Rooms) over the centuries. Next door are the elegant Pump Rooms, a splendid venue for coffee or lunch or even a glass of the fairly disgusting mineral water, straight from the pump. Any of these things can be taken accompanied by period music played by the Pump Rooms Trio.

From Abbey Church Yard turn left into Stall Street and then right along Bath Street to Cross Bath, with Hot Bath to the left, two further delightful examples of Bath's hot mineral water sources, each housed in charming 18th-century buildings. Beyond, on the right of Cross Bath, is the entrance to St John's Hospital, a medieval foundation, still offering sheltered housing.

Take the wide pavement further to the right of Cross Bath, by Chandos Buildings, and continue to Westgate Buildings. Turn right until you reach Sawclose to the right. Before continuing up there have a look at Kingsmead Square on the left, where Rosewell House is a rare example of the baroque style in this Georgian city.

Continue up Sawclose where the Theatre Royal, opened in 1805, is on the left. Next door is Popjoy's Restaurant, the former home of Beau Nash. Before crossing the road to cross into Upper Borough Walls, walk a little further beyond the restaurant and turn left along Beaufort Square, from where you can enjoy the best view of the theatre.

Along Upper Borough Walls are the surviving remnants of the medieval city wall opposite the Royal National Hospital for Rheumatic Diseases which was

The Museum of Costume houses one of the finest displays of fashion through the ages

founded in 1738. After the wall turn left down a narrow lane and then left into Trim Street, where General Wolfe's former residence is marked with a plaque. Turn right through an arch to Queen Street and left by Paxton & Whitfield into Wood Street which will bring you to Queen Square.

There are plenty of other things to see in Bath, including several notable and unusual museum collections. In Upper Town the Assembly Rooms, on Bennett Street (just off the Circus), were built to complement the Pump Room. In the basement is the Museum of Costume, which covers the history of clothes from the 16th century to the present day. Close by, at Circus Lodge, is the Museum of East Asian Art covering 7,000 years of history to include exhibits of jade, bamboo and lacquer. On the Paragon, in the Countess of Huntingdon's Chapel, is the Building of Bath Museum which is devoted to showing how the city was created, whilst next door is the British Folk Art Collection which houses a magnificent display of paintings, shop signs and rural furnishings.

The city art gallery is the Victoria Art Gallery on Bath Street. It contains a number of important paintings by British and European Masters, as well as fascinating scenes of early Bath life. There are also collections of porcelain, watches and other decorative items.

The Holburne Museum and Crafts Study Centre, a Palladian villa located at the end of Great Pulteney Street, is home to the city's finest collection of art, particularly silverware, porcelain, furniture and paintings. These treasures are displayed along with work by 20th-century artists and crafts people.

There are a number of interesting places to visit in the vicinity. Among them is Beckford's Tower, standing on the summit of Lansdown, from where there are fine views. It was built in 1825 to house part of William Beckford's art collection. Two miles (3.2km) southeast of Bath is the American Museum at Claverton Manor, a fine 19th-century house illustrating American life from the 17th to 19th centuries. The gardens include a replica of George Washington's garden at Mount Vernon.

KENNET AND AVON CANAL
The area of Bathwick and Widcombe, about the size of the rest of the other central areas combined, is also the site of the Kennet and Avon Canal, which runs through Sydney Gardens. Pleasant strolls can be had along the tow path (there is a 2-mile, 3.2-km, nature trail) and various companies also offer cruises. The canal, recently restored, was built in 1810 to link Bath with Reading, an attempt to create a more direct connection between London and the Severn, one that would be more efficient than the more northerly Thames and Severn Canal. It had, of course, the added attraction of effectively linking Reading with Bristol, since the River Avon had been made navigable between Bath and Bristol in 1727.

The Badminton Horse Trials are a precision and endurance test for both horse and rider

BADMINTON Gloucestershire Map ref ST8082

A name that most likely evokes the image of either a feathered shuttlecock and a high net or a three-day equestrian event. The first, the game of badminton which appears to have originated here in the 1870s, takes its name from Badminton House, the demesne of the Dukes of Beaufort; whilst the second is an annual event of world renown that has taken place on the estate since 1949.

Badminton House (not open), a Palladian house built for the first Duke of Beaufort in 1682, was remodelled by William Kent in 1740. It is considered a particularly fine example of the period style and the interior is wonderfully decorated. The park was partly the work of 'Capability' Brown. Some of the formal layout is on a quite extraordinary scale; the so-called Great Avenue is several miles long and lined with trees.

The 18th-century church of Great Badminton, which is in the estate grounds close to the house, is notable for its monuments to the Beaufort family, one of which, by Grinling Gibbons, is so big that the church had to be altered to accommodate it. The box pews are exceptionally large, like old-fashioned snug bars.

BEAUFORTSHIRE

The area around Badminton, seat of the Dukes of Beaufort, was known colloquially as 'Beaufortshire', since it lies in the land of the Beaufort Hunt. There is a well-known print of a chimney sweep at Chipping Sodbury saying (presumably to canvassers) 'Sorry, gentlemen, I can't vote for you 'cause I 'unts with the Duke'.

BIBURY Gloucestershire Map ref SP1106

Bibury, one of the most popular of the classic Cotswold villages, was famously described by the poet and artist William Morris as the 'most beautiful village in England', a rather risky thing to say, particularly in an area as blessed with handsome villages as the Cotswolds. Still, Bibury is undoubtedly in the first echelon, with the trout-filled Coln sliding alongside the main street, its exceptionally interesting church and an array of picturesque cottages.

Although most of what makes Bibury and Arlington (the neighbouring settlement that has become one with Bibury) so attractive dates from around the 17th century when the village prospered as a weaving centre, Bibury was a Saxon foundation. The church, in a well-tended churchyard at the heart of the original village at the far end of the main street, retains, unusually, some of its original Saxon work – the chancel arch jambs and the fragments of a cross shaft.

Among the many delightful cottages in the village, those in Arlington Row, a terrace of low gabled weavers' cottages just across the river towards the church end of the village, are the most famously photogenic. They belong to the National Trust, and are still occupied. Originally they were used by workers weaving wool for Arlington Mill at the other end of the village – they used the Rack Isle in front of the cottages, now a bird sanctuary, for drying wool. The path in front of Arlington Row continues up Awkward Hill which is lined with attractive cottages, or skirts Rack Isle, parallel to the river, to 17th-century Arlington Mill. This is now open as a museum displaying aspects of local rural life and includes a room dedicated to William Morris. Despite the popularity of the village, the future of the collection has been in some jeopardy but is likely to remain open in some form.

Next door is Bibury Trout Farm where you can catch your own fish or make purchases from the shop. Then, just across the road, is the Swan Hotel, once a fashionable haunt for the followers of Bibury Races which flourished during the 17th century. Now it is an elegant place to stay or to take afternoon tea.

A neighbouring hamlet is Ablington, a pretty collection of cottages, barns and manor houses and once the home of the Reverend Arthur Gibbs, the 19th-century author of the charming *A Cotswold Village*.

THE BISLEY PIECE

Part of Bibury churchyard is known as the Bisley Piece, the result of a curious story. It seems that at Bisley there was what was called a 'bone hole', where old bones were thrown when old graves were broken into. Some 600 years ago a priest is supposed to have fallen in and died, an incident which apparently angered the Pope himself (though quite why this should be is a mystery). Consequently he forbade burials in Bisley for two years, the residents having, instead, to bury their dead at Bibury, some 15 miles (24km) away.

The National Trust-owned cottages of Arlington Row, surely too good to be true, are still lived in

ROYAL CONNECTIONS
In the time of Charles II,
Bibury, headquarters of the
oldest racing club in Britain,
was akin to Newmarket. The
King attended the Bibury
races three times, and, in
1681, when Parliament sat at
Oxford, the spring meeting
took place here instead of
Newmarket.

DOCTOR DOOLITTLE
Castle Combe was used in
1966 as the backdrop for the
film *Doctor Doolittle* at which
time all the street lights and
television aerials were
removed and have not been
replaced.

West of Bibury on the road to Cirencester, is the
village of Barnsley. The Georgian mansion of Barnsley
Park, just outside the village, is not open to the public
although there are good walks through the grounds. In
the middle of the village, however, is Rosemary Verey's
(1918–2001) Barnsley House Garden, a lovely 18th-
century garden featuring herbs, a knot garden and a
vegetable garden planted with decorative kitchen plants.
The garden is regularly open to the public. Barnsley
church has several unusual Norman features.

South of Barnsley are the Ampneys, villages set in flat
countryside with interesting churches. Down Ampney
was the birthplace of the composer Ralph Vaughan
Williams who gave the village name to one of his best
known hymns.

CASTLE COMBE Wiltshire Map ref ST8477
This valley village, considered one of the loveliest in the
Cotswolds, is also one of the most visited and frequently
finds favour as a backdrop for period dramas.

Although its adjacent wooded hill was successively
fortified by Britons, Saxons and Normans, like most
other places in the region, Castle Combe's prosperity was
based on sheep and wool and the village was important
enough at one time to be granted the privilege of
holding a fair where wool and sheep were traded.

The village is built around the 14th-century Market
Cross with the old water pump beside it. A few yards
away are the remains of the Butter Cross which was
dismantled during the 19th century. St Andrew's Church
is probably 12th century and of particular interest inside
is the modified 15th-century clock which used to ring
the hours from the tower. The classic view of the village
is from across the bridge by the old weavers' cottages.

The small local museum is up the hill away from the
village towards the parking area. Parking is a problem
here and visitors are requested to use the car park.

*Castle Combe, familiar from
many a postcard and
period drama, is even better
in reality*

A figure representing the bounty of summer in the Roman mosaic at Chedworth

CHEDWORTH Gloucestershire Map ref SP0512

A charming village in itself, the name of Chedworth is usually associated with a Roman villa considered by many to be the finest in England. Since the two are separated by a mile or two, follow road signs to Chedworth or Chedworth Villa, depending on which you want. Chedworth village clusters quietly about a lovely old pub, opposite which a spring pours interminably, and a church that soars in comparison with the size of the village.

The villa, discovered in 1864, is owned by the National Trust, and is about a half-hour walk (or a short drive) from the village. Although the site looks perfect for a villa, it is thought that the trees which now largely surround it were not there when it was built and that the villa was, instead, in the midst of open farmland. This, and other items of information are given in the short, well-produced video which is shown every 15 minutes as part of the entry price.

Most of the original superstructure of the villa has long gone. What remains are the lower parts of the walls, enough to identify the purposes of each of the rooms, and some marvellous mosaics featuring, among other things, representations of the four seasons. Work is still in progress, and a fair amount remains to be excavated in order to get the full picture. The comparatively recent building in the middle is the administrator's house, with a small museum attached at its rear.

THE CORINIUM SCHOOL

Much of the mosaic work at Chedworth is thought to have been produced locally at Cirencester, where craftsmen had developed their own style, known as the Corinium school. Mosaic work using standard patterns was a feature common to Roman settlements throughout the empire, but, generally speaking, the later the date and the farther the settlement from Rome itself, the cruder the work. Bearing this in mind, the work produced by the Corinium school is of an unusually high standard.

Visitors enjoying the sunshine outside a popular Cirencester pub

CIRENCESTER Gloucestershire Map ref SP0201

Now a busy market town, Cirencester was once the most important city in England, after London, during the Roman occupation. Called *Corinium Dubunnorum* and founded as a military headquarters in AD 49, a number of important Roman roads radiated from the city – the Fosse Way, Ermin Street and Akeman Street. The Saxons renamed Corinium 'Cirencester' (from Coryn, meaning the top part, in reference to the River Churn, the highest source of the Thames; and Ceastre, meaning fort) but practically destroyed the town, preferring instead to build smaller settlements outside the walls. Only in the Middle Ages did Cirencester regain something of its former glory when it became the most important of the Cotswold wool towns. Markets still take place each Monday and Friday.

The town is most easily explored on foot. There are a number of well signposted car parks within easy reach of the city centre, whilst the market square is the most convenient place to begin discovery of the town.

The 15th-century parish church, one of the largest in England, is the main feature. Its magnificent Perpendicular tower was built with the reward given by Henry IV to a group of local earls who foiled a rebellion. Its fine roof is illuminated by clerestory windows, whilst the east and west windows are filled with medieval stained glass. The best-known feature of the exterior, however, is the three-storeyed south porch, overlooking the market square, which was built by the abbots in the late 15th century as an office for the abbey (now vanished) and which became the Town Hall after the Dissolution. One of the finest in the country, it was returned to the church only in the 18th century.

Inside is a painted wine-goblet style pulpit, several memorial brasses bearing the matrimonial histories of well-known wool merchants and some interesting church plate.

Opposite the church, the Tourist Information Centre is in the Victorian Corn Hall, on the market square, which also plays host to a weekly market and exhibition of local crafts. Cricklade Street, running south from the

THE KING'S HEAD

On the Market Square is the King's Head, complete with royal keystone over the door. Despite outward appearances the hotel dates back to 1340. In 1642 the Royalist Lord Chandos took refuge in the hotel, thus saving his life, whilst in 1688 Lord Lovelace, of William of Orange's army, was captured here.

square, is the site of the Brewery Arts Centre, craft studios that are housed in the old brewery.

On Park Street, northwest of the square close to Cirencester Park, is the excellent Corinium Museum which emphasises local Roman history and the many finds, including mosaics, that have been made in the area from the Roman and later eras. Many are displayed in the form of tableaux.

Close by is Thomas Street, the location of a 15th-century Weavers Hall almshouse and also Coxwell Street, lined with merchants' houses. Farther north is Spitalgate Lane, with the arcade of St John's Hospital, another group of almshouses. Due east from here is the mysterious-looking Spital Gate, all that remains of the old abbey. From here a walk through the Abbey Grounds, where remnants of the Roman walls can be seen at the eastern boundary, will take you back to the town centre.

No visit to Cirencester would be complete without a glimpse, at the very least, of Cirencester Park, probably the finest example of geometric landscaping in the country. It was the conception of the First Lord Bathurst in the early 18th century and the house (not open to the public), behind one of the largest yew hedges in the world, was built to his own design. The park was landscaped with the help of the poet Alexander Pope, among others, who has celebrated the construction of the park in verse. In fact there is a corner known as

ECCLESIASTICAL TREASURES
The church plate of Cirencester's parish church is among the most interesting in the country, particularly the Boleyn Cup which was made for Anne Boleyn, second wife of Henry VIII, in 1535. The church is notable also because it has the oldest 12-bell peal in the country, which ring out the 'pancake bell' on Shrove Tuesday.

The wide market square is dominated by the magnificent parish church, a superb example of the Perpendicular style

Pope's Seat near the polo ground. It is an excellent place for walking (the grounds are privately owned but open to walkers and riders), especially along the Broad Ride, which stretches from the entrance in Cirencester off Cecily Hill almost to Sapperton.

Apart from the wall in the Abbey Garden, the only other surviving Roman souvenir is the 2nd-century Roman Amphitheatre which, though mostly grassed over, is one of the largest and best preserved in the country. It is found on Cotswold Avenue just south of the Ring Road.

THE COLN VALLEY Gloucestershire

The River Coln, a tributary of the Thames, is arguably the prettiest of the many rivers that ripple through the Cotswolds. It rises on the escarpment not far from Cheltenham then, gently descends the slopes, passing through a number of pretty villages en route.

Withington has an unusually large church with a fine Norman doorway and a handsome wall monument to Sir John and Lady Howe of Cassey Compton. Cassey Compton is a 17th-century mansion, now a magnificent farmhouse, lying in splendid isolation in the middle of the valley, forcing the Yanworth road to curve around it. As you approach it you may, for one possibly alarming moment, see a rhinoceros in a field close by. If so it will be the product of the artist's workshop that now occupies the house. From here the river passes close to Chedworth Roman Villa (see page 71) and thence to Fossbridge, a steep point on the Roman Fosse Way where an ancient inn continues to attract passing customers. On the other side of the road the Coln furrows across the meadows of Coln St Dennis, a small, silent village built around a small green, with a small church. Look for the mysterious inscription to Joan Burton on the interior wall of the tower, as well as the Norman corbel stones that now line the nave.

The River Coln meanders through leafy meadows at Coln St Dennis

Further on is the pretty hamlet of Calcot and then almost immediately Coln Rogers with a church remarkable for its Saxon plan and Saxon window north of the chancel. Winson comes next. At the old mill, where the road zigzags, there are charming gardens; towards the centre are converted barns whilst the compact green is overlooked by a classical looking manor house. After Winson come Ablington and Bibury (see pages 69 and 68).

Finally, before going on to Fairford and Lechlade (see pages 80 and 81), the Coln arrives at Coln St Aldwyns, where the green is shaded by a magnificent horse chestnut tree and the New Inn is a fine pub. A pretty churchyard surrounds the church which has memorial windows commemorating John Keble, the 19th-century reformer, and his father.

JAMES GIBBS
The Manor House at Winson is an unexpected piece of classical architecture in the middle of Cotswold vernacular. Its architect was eminent in his field, for James Gibbs designed the Radcliffe Library in Oxford and St Bartholomew's Hospital in London, where the owner of the manor, Surgeon General Howes, was well known.

THE DUNTISBOURNES Gloucestershire
Map ref SO9607

A string of villages along the small River Dunt just to the north of Cirencester, the Duntisbournes have a special character on account of their saddleback church towers which have something almost French about them.

Duntisbourne Abbotts was the home of Dr Matthew Baillie, the royal physician who attended George III during his many years of mental illness. Cotswold Farm was the home of the 19th-century Methodist, Elizabeth Cross, who set up a mission in Tonga and converted the Tonga royal family.

Duntisbourne Leer is prettily forded by the Dunt, as is Middle Duntisbourne, barely more than a farm at the bottom of a steep valley. The church at Duntisbourne Rouse has a particularly dramatic situation at the top of a slope leading down to the Dunt and an atmospheric interior with box pews and medieval wall paintings.

The pleasingly low church at Duntisbourne Abbotts huddles in the churchyard

ECCLESIASTICAL OWNERS
Duntisbourne Abbotts was once owned by the abbots of Gloucester; whilst Duntisbourne Leer belonged to the abbey of Lire, in Normandy, until 1416.

Twelve high arches support the old Market House and Town Hall at Dursley

DURSLEY Gloucestershire Map ref ST7598
Although this busy market town just beneath the Cotswold edge has been quite severely modernised in places, its old centre remains intact and boasts some interesting items. Nestling just beneath wooded slopes, it was once an important cloth manufacturing town and the delightfully arcaded market hall, built in 1729, and town hall sit bang in the centre, complete with statue of Queen Anne.

The church is not blessed with a very harmonious interior – though there is a chapel of 1450, built by the merchant Thomas Tanner – but does have a fine vaulted porch in the Perpendicular style. The tower in Gothic style was only rebuilt at the beginning of the 18th century with a grant from Queen Anne after the spire collapsed in 1698 as the bells were rung in celebration of not long-completed repairs. The north door of the church was blocked to prevent it being used as a right of way, much used by the citizenry for the collection of water from the Broad Well. Although in the immediate area Woodmancote offers a better selection of 18th-century houses, Dursley is a pleasant, old fashioned sort of place and exploration of its small centre is certainly rewarding.

The village of Cam, just to the north of Dursley, still has a single factory producing high quality cloth, mostly for dress uniforms and for snooker table coverings. Cam church, apparently built by Lord Berkeley to save his soul after the murder of Edward II at Berkeley Castle, contains a Jacobean pulpit. The nearby Cam Peak and Cam Long Down are Cotswold outliers, which clearly show their geological formation, the softer rock having eroded around them.

To the northwest of Dursley is Stinchcombe Hill, the most westerly point of the Cotswolds, from where there are wonderful views along the escarpment.

WILLIAM TYNDALE
Southwest of Dursley is Nibley Knoll with its distinctive needle-shaped monolith rising out of the hillside. This is the Tyndale Monument, built in 1886 in honour of William Tyndale, born in nearby North Nibley, and the first man, in 1484, to translate the Bible from Latin into English. It is possible to climb its 111 feet (34m) if you so desire, from where there are, of course, excellent views. Tyndale was martyred in Flanders in 1536.

DYRHAM Somerset Map ref ST7475

A short distance to the north of Bath is Dyrham, a picturesque village bearing a name that is associated with a battle of enormous consequence for Britain. It was here, on nearby Hinton Hill, in AD 577 that the invading Anglo-Saxons (from the established kingdom of Wessex) finally defeated the Britons, forcing them for ever into the mountains of Wales and permitting the capture of the Romano-Briton cities of Bath, Cirencester and Gloucester. Hinton Hill is covered in medieval plough furrows but of the battle, one of the most significant in English history, there is no trace.

Dyrham Park, close to the church, was a Tudor house substantially rebuilt at the end of the 17th century to a design by Talman for William Blathwayt, a Secretary of State to William III and 'a very proper, handsome person, very dextrous in business', and who, 'besides all this, has married a great fortune'. Now a National Trust property, it contains magnificent collections of china and Dutch paintings of the period, a reflection of the regular journeys that Blathwayt made to Holland in the company of William III. In the garden is one of the earliest-known greenhouses, whilst all that remains of the once elaborate water garden in the formal Dutch style is a statue of Neptune.

A herd of fallow deer now grazes in the parkland, as deer have done since Saxon times, though now the park rejoices in the more naturalistic English style, designed by the great landscape architect Humphry Repton. In 1993 the house was used as a backdrop for the film *Remains of the Day* which starred Sir Anthony Hopkins.

THOMAS KEY

Cold Ashton lies just south of Dyrham. The 16th-century church here was built, unusually, by the rector. His name was Thomas Key and his mark, a T and a key, is much in evidence. How it came to pass that a humble rector should be in a position to rebuild a parish church is an open question.

While the parkland is open all year, the house at Dyrham Park is closed to visitors during the winter

Keble Country

An interesting short ramble exploring three charming villages that have links with the great 19th-century church reformer, John Keble. Part of the walk follows the picturesque River Leach. It may be muddy in places after rain, but the going is generally firm.

Time: 2½ hours. Distance: 4¼ miles (6.8km).
Location: 3½ miles (5.6km) northeast of Fairford.
Start: Southrop village, situated off the A417 Cirencester to Faringdon road, northeast of Fairford; or 2 miles (3.2km) off the A361 Lechlade to Burford road, north of Lechlade. Park in the village street, close to the Swan Inn. (OS grid ref: SP201035.)
OS Map: Outdoor Leisure 45 (The Cotswolds) 1:25,000.
See Key to Walks on page 121.

ROUTE DIRECTIONS

From **Southrop**, with the pub on your right, walk along the road in the direction of Fairford. Pass the village hall, the road to Lechlade and the old well and continue for a quarter of a mile (0.4km) to a junction by a house. Proceed straight across on to a green lane, passing Tiltup Farm. The path undulates through trees. Keep ahead to eventually reach a gate and an opening into a field on the right. Turn right here and follow the right-hand side of the field to the other side. Pass to the right of a pair of old circular grain dryers and continue until you come to a bridle gate at a road.

Turn right, descend between hedgerows into Hammersmith Bottom, then as it levels out, turn right into a field. Keep to its left-hand edge, following the curve of the field, then go through a gate on the left and maintain direction to the top of this field, and cross a narrow bridge (may be overgrown). Join a short path to the field corner, keep straight on towards woodland and follow a wide track to the left of the trees and a stone wall, then continue to a road beyond farm buildings.

Turn left and descend into **Eastleach Turville**. At a junction by the clocktower, turn second right through the village and curve left by the war memorial down to the river. Cross the old clapper bridge (Keble Bridge) over the River Leach and follow the path into **Eastleach Martin** churchyard. Pass the church on your left, go through a gate, turn right and continue along a road.

Remain on the lane, parallel with the river for over half a mile (0.8km), then where it veers left away from the river, bear off right to a stile and follow the path beside the river towards Fyfield which is on your left.

Cross a wooden bridge stile and proceed to traverse a stone bridge on the right across the river. Continue ahead, uphill through a meadow, towards the village of Southrop, soon to bear diagonally left to a stile in the top left-hand corner of the meadow. Walk along a passage between a house and

Children enjoying the shallows by Keble Bridge, at Eastleach

dovecot to a road and turn left to reach the Swan and your car.

POINTS OF INTEREST

Southrop

An interesting village that boasts a fine16th-century manor house, a carefully restored 17th-century corn mill and the tiny, Norman Church of St Peter. The church has no tower but features a magnificent font, carved with the five Virtues trampling on the five Vices, the names of which are written backwards. The north and south walls of the nave are patterned in the herringbone style of late Saxon type.

John Keble, leader of the 19th-century Oxford Movement, was curate here between 1823 and 1825. Here he wrote much of his volume of verse *The Christian Year* which was to become an Anglican High Church *vade mecum*. He was also responsible, it is thought, for the rediscovery of the Norman font, which had been built into the south doorway.

Eastleach Turville and Eastleach Martin

A pair of villages, Eastleach Turville is the larger, separated by the River Leach. Each village has its own church (although Saint Michael and Saint Martin, Eastleach Martin, has been redundant since 1982), which stand within sight of each other across the river.

Eastleach Martin was also known as Bouthrop, a name

The little church at Eastleach Martin is tucked away in the trees

which predates the Norman conquest. John Keble was born at nearby Fairford. He was curate of both parishes in the 19th century. The shape of his church seems to have changed little and it boasts some ancient bells, one of which was cast in about 1400.

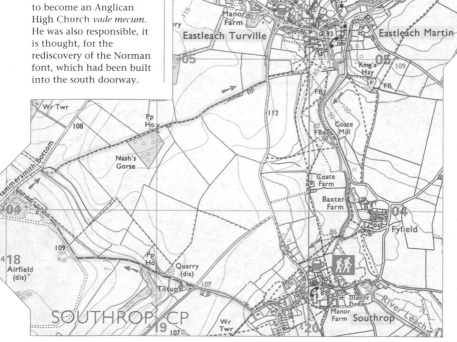

*Medieval stained glass in
the church at Fairford
vividly portrays the Passion*

LORD OF THE MANOR
The influence of the Tame
family and the proximity of
the river led Henry VIII's
librarian, John Leland, to
observe: 'Fairforde never
flourished afore ye Tames
came to it'. Wealthy wool
merchant John Tame, who
built the church, became
Fairford's lord of the manor.
His son, Sir Edmund Tame,
was also a church builder and
is responsible for St Peter's at
Rendcomb, 5 miles (8km)
north of Cirencester, where
his initials can be found on
some of the corbels and on
some old glass in a nave
window. It is thought, too,
that the church tower at
Barnsley was largely the result
of his patronage.

FAIRFORD Gloucestershire Map ref SP1501
In our epoch Fairford is most often thought of in
connection with the supersonic airliner *Concorde*, which
had its maiden flight at the military airfield here. But
Fairford is rather more than that. Located on the River
Coln and the A417, Fairford is another of those towns
that has a busy lowland feel that does not seem entirely
of the Cotswolds.

The focal point of the village, wherein lies the fragile
object of its fame, is its magnificent late Perpendicular
Church of St Mary, largely rebuilt from 1497 by John
Tame and his son Edmund, the most influential of
Fairford's medieval wool merchants. The church is
dominated by a central tower supported by massive
pillars within; but its greatest glory is the medieval
stained-glass windows, the only complete set in the
country, which narrate the highlights of the Biblical
story. They are most likely the work of the Flanders
craftsman, Barnard Flower, whom Henry VIII employed
to glaze the windows of King's College Chapel,
Cambridge and the Lady Chapel, Westminster Abbey,
and who was almost certainly helped by English and
French craftsmen. The great west window, in particular,
which shows the Last Judgement, is of riveting,
luminous beauty. Not to be missed either are the
amusing carved misericords underneath the choir stalls.

In the churchyard are buried two distinguished locals –
Valentine Strong, of the eminent family of stone
quarriers of Taynton; and Tiddles, the church cat.

Next to the church is the old school of 1738. The
church itself overlooks the water meadows and the old
mill by a picturesque bridge. From the church a pleasant
circuit is possible which will bring you back to the main
street. Most of the houses that line the street are 17th or
18th century and, along with the many inns, are a
reminder of Fairford's importance as a coaching town.
John Keble, the 19th-century church reformer, was born
at Keble House, on the north side of the road at the east
end of the town.

To the north of Fairford are twin villages – Eastleach
Turville and Eastleach Martin (see Walk on page 78).

LECHLADE Gloucestershire Map ref SU2199
Another town with that peculiar quality which derives
more from its rivers, notably the Thames, than from the
Cotswolds. In the Middle Ages it was on the Salt Way
but it is very much a river town, being at the confluence
of three – the Coln, the Leach and the Thames – and it
was at Lechlade that the stone quarried at Taynton was
loaded before setting out for London, where it was to be
used in the construction of St Paul's Cathedral. From
1789 the Thames was linked to the Severn via the
Thames and Severn Canal which started close to here, to
the southeast at Inglesham, where the old round house,
built for the canal lengthmen (responsible for the
maintenance of certain lengths of the canal), still stands.

Where there are rivers there are bridges. Just south of
the town, the A361 crosses the Thames with the old
tollbridge, the 18th-century Halfpenny (or Ha'penny)
Bridge; whilst to the east the A417 crosses the Thames by
means of the 13th-century St John Bridge where a statue
of Father Thames presides close to the Thames' highest
lock and from where there is a fine view of the town.

Lechlade is built about its Market Square, and its wool
church. The square, and the streets that radiate from it –
Burford Street, High Street and St John Street – are
overlooked by a fine collection of 17th- to 19th-century
buildings. The church, with its distinctive spire, dates
from the late 15th century when it was built largely from
the same quarries at Taynton that later provided the
stone for St Paul's. It contains an east window from 1510
and the brass of wool merchant, John Townsend, as well
as a fine chancel roof. One balmy summer evening in

PERCY SHELLEY
Shelley came to be inspired by
Lechlade's church in 1815
merely by chance. He, in the
company of the satirist
Thomas Love Peacock, author
of *Nightmare Abbey*, and his
young mistress Mary Goodwin
who was later to become his
wife, had rowed to Lechlade
from Old Windsor. The plan
had been to reach the source
of the Thames but in fact they
got no farther than Lechlade
where they stayed in an inn
where Shelley, poetic musings
notwithstanding, managed to
consume 'three mutton
chops, well peppered'. The
next day the trio returned to
Old Windsor.

*Pleasure craft leaving St
John's Lock, on the River
Thames, with the spire of
Lechlade church behind*

1815 the church inspired the Romantic poet Percy Shelley to write:

'Thou too, aerial pile! Whose pinnacles
Point from one shrine like pyramids of fire'

The bustle of commercial river life has long gone from Lechlade, although pleasure craft still bring colour and movement and it is possible to hire small boats from the boatyard near the Ha'penny Bridge. The walk along the Thames, southwest from the Ha'penny Bridge, is very enjoyable and at Inglesham there is a very pretty church by the river, restored by William Morris.

Just to the southeast of Lechlade is Buscot Park, a handsome 18th-century house, with a well-known series of paintings by Burne-Jones in the saloon, and a trio of Rembrandts among many other other works of art reflecting the taste of the First Lord Faringdon. The house is set in an attractive park close to the village of Buscot, with its interesting church and 18th-century parsonage which is open to the public.

MINCHINHAMPTON Gloucestershire Map ref SO8700
Overlooking the Stroud Valley on the fringe of the eponymous common, Minchinhampton, one of the most important cloth towns of south Gloucestershire by the 18th century, easily goes unheeded. It was a town of small traders unable to withstand the various crashes that periodically afflicted the industry, and so finally relapsing to a rural calm. Indeed, the church's truncated tower may be explained by the absence of wealthy patrons to replace the earlier, decayed spire.

It deserves a look, however, for it is an attractive wool town built around the old Market Square. Here you will find the 17th-century Market House balanced on stone pillars and, unusually, the post office residing in a Queen Anne building.

MINCHINHAMPTON COMMON
The common has several historical associations. After it was granted to the people of Minchinhampton in the 16th century, any weaver was permitted to enclose land here and build a home. The bulwarks are the remains of an Iron-Age fort, and the possible base for the resistance to the Romans led by Caratacus; whilst Whitfield's Tump is a barrow from where George Whitfield, the Gloucester-born Methodist preacher addressed a 20,000 strong congregation in 1743. During World War I the common was used as an airfield, manned by Australian airmen.

Minchinhampton's truncated church spire gives the village a curiously Gothic air

The elegant little post office in Minchinhampton is worth a second look

The church, just apart from the square, dates back to the 12th century. It contains a particularly fine set of brasses, whilst the 14th-century south transept contains a stately array of tombs and effigies.

The common is 600 acres of National Trust owned turf. A wide, windswept expanse of grassland, fringed with the villages of the Frome and Nailsworth valleys, a circumnavigation of the common is rewarding for the views that it reveals.

Amberley, the village on the west side of the common, is featured in the Victorian novel, *John Halifax, Gentleman* by Mrs Craik. She lived at Rose Cottage.

NORTHLEACH Gloucestershire Map ref SP1114

One of the most important of the wool towns in the Middle Ages, Northleach retains something of the flavour of that period, with its market square overlooked by one of the finest wool churches in the Cotswolds, all fortunately now bypassed by the A40, replacing the old coaching route which in the past ran through the town. The High Street is an interesting mixture of houses of all periods, some of which, unusually, are half-timbered and most of which reflect the burgage plots (see panel) that belonged to the merchants of yore.

One of these buildings, just east of the market place, is now Keith Harding's World of Mechanical Music, in what was the old school. This is a fascinating place, a shop as you go in, but beyond it a collection of clocks and mechanical instruments from all over Europe, ranging from barrel organs to pianolas. Many of these

BURGAGE PLOTS
Burgage plots were created to enable the maximum number of shops to line the main street. Northleach Borough was established by the Abbey of St Peter, in Gloucester, in 1226. The annual rents were one shilling (5p) for a burgage plot, 6d (2½p) for a market stall and 1d for a cottage.

An eclectic collection at the World of Mechanical Music

THE WOOL INDUSTRY
The church at Northleach is one of the great testaments to what made the Cotswolds famous – the wool industry.

Domestic wool weaving was important during the Roman period, whilst Saxon weavers' huts have been found in Bourton-on-the-Water. But it was during the Middle Ages that wool became an industry famous throughout Europe. By the 13th century most of the grazing land was owned by the great abbeys at Worcester, Tewkesbury and Winchcombe. The 14th-century Florentine merchant, Peglotti, thought Winchcombe Abbey to be one of the top 12 wool producers in England. By 1360 England was exporting 32,000 sacks per year of finest wool, much of it produced by the local breed, known as the 'Cotswold lion' because of its mane-like fleece.

As cloth started to be woven in England, so dawned the era of the great cloth merchants like the Tames at Fairford and the Forteys and Midwinters at Northleach. Their wealth was an important factor in the construction of wool churches.

Wool continued to be important, but by 1800 it was sold direct to clothiers, making the great markets redundant. The reasons for the sudden decline of the Cotswold wool-cloth industry after this period are open to debate, but certainly one factor was the abundance of coal in the north, used to power the new steam mills.

are frequently demonstrated, whilst some of the restored items are for sale.

Behind the square, among a little network of lanes about the old mill, is the most striking building in the town, its wool church which, as it stands, dates from the 15th century. A very fine example of the English Perpendicular style, it is particularly noted for its magnificent south porch, one of the finest in the country. The interior is quite stark but beautifully proportioned and contains the grandest collection of monumental brasses in the Cotswolds, commemorating the medieval wool merchants who brought prosperity to Northleach and whose money built the church.

There are two sets of almshouses, one at Mill End, another at East End. At the western end of the town the High Street meets the Roman Fosse Way. On the other side of the road is an 18th-century building that was originally a prison and is now the Cotswold Countryside Collection. The prison was built by Sir William Blackburn according to the ideas of the philanthropist Sir George Onesiphorus Paul, a member of an eminent family of Woodchester clothiers. The courthouse was in use until 1974 and part of the museum consists of a reconstruction of an 18th-century cell block, but most is devoted to a display of facets of traditional rural life. There is a fine collection of Gloucestershire farm wagons.

A short drive (or walk) to the northwest is the hamlet of Hampnett, which has an exceptionally interesting Norman church with carved birds on the chancel arch and Victorian stencilling.

PAINSWICK Gloucestershire Map ref SO8609
'The Queen of the Cotswolds' sits more or less at the point of transition from the northern to the southern Cotswolds. Perched regally at the edge of the steep slopes of the Painswick Valley, the town is a hive of activity about the little network of lanes around the church. It is the most Dickensian of Cotswold villages.

Like other important towns in this part of the Cotswolds, Painswick's prosperity reached its acme in the 17th and 18th centuries when the stream below was harnessed to work the mills producing wool cloth. The purity of the water also meant that cloth dyeing became important. The character of the village depends considerably on the fine houses built by the wealthy wool merchants of the era.

But the most striking feature of Painswick is the graceful 17th-century spire of the church. The church itself is mainly 15th century and contains some interesting monuments, although it is the churchyard for which Painswick is especially noted. There are two reasons for this. The most striking features are the clipped colonnades of yew, which have graced the churchyard since 1792. There are said to be only 99, since the Devil always kills off the hundredth, and indeed, it is now impossible to count them with ease since some have become intertwined with each other. The other distinction is the congregation of table tombs from the 17th and 18th centuries, many of which were carved by a local mason, Joseph Bryan, and his two sons.

Stroll around the heart of the town and along Bisley Street, the original main street and the oldest part of the town. Here you will find the Little Fleece, now a National Trust bookshop in a largely 17th-century house that was built onto the 14th-century Fleece Inn.

Just outside the town, on the Gloucester road, is Painswick Rococo Garden, the landscaped 18th-century garden around Painswick House. It is utterly charming, particularly in early spring when snowdrops flower in abundance. Near by is Painswick Beacon, site of an Iron-Age fort and now of a golf course, from where there are tremendous views across the plain to Gloucester.

The neighbouring villages of Sheepscombe (see Walk on page 86) and Slad are noted for their associations with the author Laurie Lee.

THE CLYPPING CEREMONY

The Clypping Ceremony at Painswick church has nothing to do with pruning the famous yew trees in the churchyard but derives from the Old English word 'clyppan', meaning to embrace. It takes place every 19 September, or the nearest Sunday to that date, in association with the Feast of the Nativity of St Mary. In the afternoon the children involved in the ceremony join hands to form a circle around the church, approach the church and retreat three times as they sing a traditional hymn. A special cake is also baked – known as 'puppy dog pie', it contains a small china dog, a reminder, perhaps, of the pagan origins of the festivity.

Caught in the evening sunlight, Painswick, seen from Edge

Through Ancient Woodland

This delightful walk begins in the scattered village of Cranham, passes through ancient woodland and skirts the lovely village of Sheepscombe, celebrated in Laurie Lee's novel, 'Cider with Rosie'. Mainly firm woodland paths and no major climbs.

Time: 2½ hours. Distance: 3½ miles (5.6km).
Location: 6 miles (9.7km) southeast of Gloucester.
Start: Cranham village, situated off the A46 Cheltenham to Stroud road, 3 miles (4.8km) north of Painswick. Park off the road near Cranham School.
(OS grid ref: SO893125.)
OS Map: Explorer 179 (Cheltenham, Gloucester & Stroud) 1:25,000.
See Key to Walks on page 121.

ROUTE DIRECTIONS

From **Cranham**, take the dark track to the left of the school on to Cranham Common, then shortly turn right at a crossing of paths and follow a track behind the school with the common on the left. Descend towards woodland, then just before the entrance to a trout farm, turn left and follow a path downhill and across a stream.

Ascend to a gate and join a path that climbs through Saltridge Common Wood (nature reserve). On reaching a crossroads, take the left-hand path which rises through trees (possible blue arrows), then climb steeply into a small clearing and junction of paths. Continue straight on, uphill, the path finally levelling out at the woodland fringe. Bear right between a stone wall and the wood, and proceed for nearly half a mile (0.8km), disregarding all paths leading into the wood. Eventually descend steadily to reach a crossing of paths.

Pass through the gate ahead not marked 'private' and turn left into Lord's and Lady's Woods (NT). Almost immediately, keep right at a fork and descend the arrowed path through the wood. Pass a further NT sign, ignore a path right, and head uphill with a field visible to your left. Shortly, at a junction of paths – one leads down into **Sheepscombe** – take the more defined path in front of you leading out of the wood on to an area of rough grassland (from here there are fine views towards Painswick). Keep left, following the track around the wood and descend, then on nearing a house, bear left on a narrow path to a gate and stile. Cross a field to a stile in the top

Ancient beech woods at Cranham offer shady summer walking

A pleasing blend of old and new houses in Cotswold stone at Sheepscombe

right-hand corner, then follow a woodland path for 100 yards (91m) to a cross path. Proceed ahead, then keep to the main path by a stone wall and soon descend with Ebworth House above you to the left. Just before reaching a path merging from the right, bear left up a steep path, leading to a farm track at the top of the ridge.

Turn left, pass through a farmyard, a gate in a stone wall and a wooden gate by a track beyond. Enter a further field and head for a stile in the top left-hand corner. Go through some trees, climb a stile and bear diagonally right, keeping left of a clump of trees, to a stile near a gate in a hedge. Maintain direction to a gap in a hedge next to a tree, and walk straight ahead, with Overtown on your right. Turn sharp right by the second tree (house to the right), and head down the field, across a stream, and through a gate into woodland. Follow a clear path back to Cranham Common and the start point.

POINTS OF INTEREST

Cranham

The Church of St James, with its very attractive interior, is mostly 15th century and has several notable features, such as a 16th-century rood screen, a fine monument to the long serving 18th-century rector, Obadiah Done, and a handsome altar tryptych. The importance of sheep and wool to the prosperity of the area in days gone by is commemorated by the carving of shears on the tower. The village is noted for its annual feast and ox roast.

Sheepscombe

An unspoilt village, beautifully situated in a peaceful valley. Like many of the villages in the area it was once, as its name suggests, dependent on sheep and the wool industry, and its old mill still stands. The church, which is Victorian, is rather a curiosity, with its tiny, almost symbolic, tower.

Sheepscombe, like its near neighbour, Slad, is associated with the author Laurie Lee, and particularly with his childhood autobiography, *Cider With Rosie*, in which the attractive village is frequently mentioned.

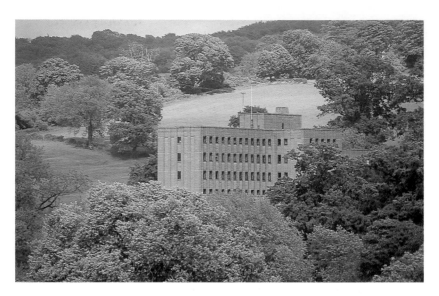

The startling modernity of Prinknash Abbey is a reminder that abbey life continues in the present day

PRINKNASH ABBEY POTTERY
Rich beds of clay were discovered when foundations were being dug for the new building, and so the pottery at Prinknash was established. It has a distinctive style and is sold in many parts of the world. The monks are skilled in other crafts as well, and make many items for the abbey church.

PRINKNASH Gloucestershire Map ref SO8814

Close to Painswick on the sheltered slopes beneath Cranham Woods is a building which, despite looking like a huge cinema, just about succeeds in blending in with its surroundings, a testament to the use of good building materials, in this case stone from the quarries around Guiting. Prinknash (pronounced 'Prinash'), a Benedictine house, is one of Britain's few abbeys. The 14th-century foundation, a hunting lodge for the abbots of Gloucester, became a manor house and chapel and was used as his headquarters by Prince Rupert during the Siege of Gloucester, is still visible across the valley. Its location was celebrated by Horace Walpole who, in 1714, described it as 'commanding Elysium'. The last private owner was a Catholic who invited the monks to move here from Caldey Island, off the Welsh coast. The current building was begun in 1939.

The abbey is worth visiting. Apart from the views, the tearoom, the abbey church and the gardens, the abbey has made use of the clay in the area to establish a pottery of repute. The nearby Bird Park is well stocked with birds, goats and deer.

THE SODBURYS Gloucestershire Map ref ST7282

There are in fact three Sodburys, Little, Old and Chipping, scattered around narrow lanes down the Cotswold escarpment, with a remote character that hardly seems Cotswold and in fact has more in common with the vale. Chipping Sodbury (Chipping, as elsewhere, here means 'market') is the newest of the villages, deliberately established to become a market town in 1227, whereas Old Sodbury, the original, has an ancient church and a British encampment above the town from where there are magnificent views.

Little Sodbury is the most interesting of the three. Small as it is, this village has substantial historical associations. The manor house, with its quite astounding 15th-century Great Hall, played host to Henry VIII and Anne Boleyn; and William Tyndale, the first man to translate the Bible into English, was employed here as a tutor and chaplain in 1521 until his plans and ideas, compelled him to move abroad.

The church, dedicated to St Adeline, originally stood next to the manor house but was moved to its present site when urgent repairs had to be carried out. Near the Sodburys is the Somerset, or Hawkesbury, Monument, which commemorates Lord Edward Somerset, one of the Badminton Beauforts, who served at the Battle of Waterloo with exceptional gallantry for which he received particular thanks from Parliament.

SOUTH CERNEY AND THE COTSWOLD WATER PARK Gloucestershire Map ref SU0497

South Cerney, 3 miles (4.8km) south-east of Cirencester, is situated on the banks of the Churn where you will find an 18th-century octagonal gazebo and, nearby, along Silver Street and Church Lane, are rows of attractive houses. The church has a Norman south doorway above which are sculptures reflecting Heaven and Hell, whilst within are the remains of a 12th-century crucifix, one of the earliest wood carvings in the country.

The old Thames and Severn Canal passes just to the north of the village and walks along the towpath are possible; but the village is best known, nowadays, for the series of flooded gravel pits that make up the Cotswold Water Park. Broadly speaking there are two sections, one between Cricklade and Kemble (where South Cerney is situated), the other between Fairford and Lechlade, which provide facilities for nature lovers and sportsmen alike. There are three nature reserves and the wetlands attract millions of wildfowl, particularly in the winter. The various activities coexist happily on the 100 lakes.

ST ADELINE'S CHURCH
The small church of Little Sodbury is the only one in the country dedicated to St Adeline. There are two possible explanations for the dedication, either because the first Norman lord of the manor came from an area of Normandy where there was a convent founded by the saint; or because she was the patron saint of Flemish weavers who worked in the area.

The extensive pools of the Cotswolds Water Park attract sporting types and birdwatchers in equal numbers

THE ARTS AND CRAFTS MOVEMENT

The Arts and Crafts Movement, which was a London and Cotswold phenomenon, was a 19th-century aesthetic and social movement instigated by the art critic John Ruskin and the artist and poet William Morris as a constructive protest against the mass-produced excesses of the Industrial Revolution. A company, Morris & Co., was established to produce handmade furniture, glass, wallpapers and textiles. It looked to the Middle Ages for its ideal and liked to concentrate on fine materials, solid craftsmanship and expertise and a certain simplicity of style that was both rustic and courtly, of universal appeal. Later, in 1888, Morris helped the artist and designer C R Ashbee to found the Guild and School of Arts and Crafts, but production costs led to its early demise. However, some of the designs, particularly for textiles and wallpaper, remain popular and the tradition of quality workmanship continues to inspire craftsmen in the area.

THE STROUD VALLEY Gloucestershire

For a small area, the Cotswolds reveal remarkable diversity, but the Stroud Valley possesses a singular character, much dependent on its depth, narrow base and serpentine course. Stroud itself is at the head of the valley which runs east close to Cirencester, a number of other valleys feeding it from north and south.

Its character is also dependent upon its history as the manufacturing centre of the Cotswolds, with its fast-flowing streams and the mills that straddled them. Stroud became the centre of the wool industry from the 15th century as cloth supplanted fleeces in importance. With industrialisation during the 18th and 19th centuries the valley bristled with mills. There were 150 of them at one time, before decline set in as the industry moved away to Yorkshire, leaving only two companies producing high-quality cloth for dress uniforms.

Stroud is spread a little like a cloth over the Cotswold slopes. Of no great beauty, it is nonetheless a bustling town of considerable interest, centred in the area around the High Street, close to which you will find the Shambles, the former meat market, and the Tudor Town Hall. Close by, on George Street, are the handsome 19th-century Subscription Rooms, home to the Tourist Information Centre. The Stroud District Museum, situated next to the Stratford Park Leisure Centre, offers an excellent insight into the history of the area and displays, among other items, a collection of early lawnmowers (the inventor of the lawnmower, Mr Budding, was from this valley).

There are some good walks to be had along the Stroudwater Canal. Now disused, it was the more successful part of the Thames and Severn Canal system, functioning until 1954.

Southwest of Stroud is Selsley Common and Selsley, with its church of particular interest for its stained glass by William Morris, Dante Gabriel Rossetti, Edward Burne-Jones, Philip Webb and Ford Madox Brown. Just farther west, near Stonehouse, is one of the area's pre-industrial legacies, Frocester Tithe Barn, believed to be one of the finest in England.

To the east of Stroud is Chalford, its houses on steep lanes and along terraces and shelves of the north slope of the valley. A legacy of the Industrial Revolution, its houses were built by the clothiers and merchants making their fortune during the 18th and 19th centuries and by weavers working first from home and later at the mills which still line the Thames and Severn Canal. The 18th-century church contains several items produced by members of the Arts and Crafts Movement.

The Thames and Severn Canal, today the subject of a new and controversial restoration project, was one of those great Victorian enterprises that was magnificent in conception but almost redundant by the time of its realisation. Completed in 1789, to facilitate trade

The restored entrance to the Coates Tunnel suggests a grandeur and importance never quite achieved on this backwater of a canal

between the two rivers that were also important commercial waterways, the number of locks, difficulties with the 2¼ mile Sapperton Tunnel and a shortage of water engendered constant problems. Other, better, canals and the arrival of the railways put paid to it and the last recorded journey was made in 1911. The two temple-like tunnel portals are visible at Coates and Daneway where the pubs, built for the boatmen, still function. A stroll along the old canal is recommended, as indeed is a visit to Sapperton, a village that was the home of Ernest Gimson and the Barnsley brothers, of the Arts and Crafts Movement.

Just to the north of Chalford is the delightful village of Bisley (see Walk on page 92), with pubs and a church that has a dramatic spire and a unique 'Poor Soul's Light', a 13th-century structure which contained candles lit during masses for the poor.

To the south of Stroud is Woodchester where the churchyard is the site of a Roman villa with a magnificent mosaic.

RODBOROUGH COMMON
Rodborough Common is just to the south-west of Stroud. A good place for walking, the common is also the site of Rodborough Fort, built in 1761 as a pleasure-house by George Hawker, a local dyer. It was rebuilt in Victorian style in 1870.

A Ramble From Bisley

From the beautiful village of Bisley, this long and varied ramble follows undulating field paths, woodland tracks, quiet narrow lanes and a romantic stretch of the overgrown Thames and Severn Canal.

Time: 4½ hours. Distance: 8 miles (12.9km).
Location: 4 miles (6.4km) east of Stroud.
Start: Bisley village, signposted off the B4070 Stroud to Birdlip road, 2 miles (3.2km) northeast of Stroud. Park in the main village street, near the post office.
(OS grid ref: SO905059.)
OS Map: Explorer 168 (Stroud, Tetbury & Malmesbury)
1:25,000
See Key to Walks on page 121.

ROUTE DIRECTIONS

Face **Bisley** post office and turn right along the main street. Near its end, turn left up a short and steep lane, cross the road on to another lane and follow it sharp right, passing Rectory Farm on your left. Take the waymarked path right, through a gate, keep to the left of a field to a gate, and proceed to the right of the next field to a lane.

Climb the stile opposite, then bear diagonally left across a meadow to a stile near its corner. Maintain direction across the next field, cross a stile, then head straight across the following field to a stile. Bear right across a field surrounded by high hedges and go through a break in the hedge. Turn right, bear left around the field edge to a stile on the right, just before the field corner. Head straight across a rough meadow, with farm buildings visible to your right, to a stile, then descend past trees to a stile on the edge of woodland. Proceed steeply downhill through the trees, bear slightly right across another meadow, towards Bournes Green, to a stile beside a wall.

Join a path that bears right between a wall and fence to a stile, then bear left past cottages to a clearing and a lane. Turn right, keep left at a junction, then at the next junction, bear left (unsuitable for heavy vehicles) steeply downhill. Ascend, then at a sharp bend beyond Lillyhorn Farm, cross a stile on the right and walk straight across a grassy valley slope into another field.

The walk starts at Bisley post office, a hub of village activities

Turn left towards houses and locate an alleyway leading to a road in **Oakridge**. Turn left, then immediately right downhill, ignore a left turn by the old well and take the next left. Pass some cottages, bear right uphill, then, as the road levels, turn right over a stile and bear

diagonally left across a field to a gate to the right of a house. Turn left along a path through two fields, via stiles, to a road. Keep ahead, bear sharp right and descend for half a mile (0.8km) to cross an old brick bridge then turn left along the right bank of the overgrown Thames and Severn Canal. Cross to the left bank and continue to a road, opposite the **Daneway** Inn.

Turn left, bear right behind the pub, then just beyond the entrance to Daneway House, climb the stile on the left and head steeply uphill. Bear right towards trees, go through a gate at the top, then keep to the left margin of a field to a gate and a lane beside a house. Turn left, then, after half a mile (0.8km), keep right at a junction and shortly take the arrowed path right, opposite Frith House, into a paddock.

Bear left into a field, head diagonally right to a stile and join a woodland path to a junction by a stone bridge. Bear left, then at a junction of paths near a house head right, continuing steeply through woodland to a stile. Bear right across a meadow to a gate and lane. Turn right downhill, keeping left at a fork on to a track, bear left at a spinney to pass several fields, climb a stile on the right and bear half-left across two fields to a stile and road. Turn right, then at the corner, cross to a defile into a field and return to the start point at Bisley.

POINTS OF INTEREST

Bisley

A handsome south Cotswold upland village that became prosperous as a result of the cloth trade. There are some fine houses in the village and the church has a magnificent spire and a 13th-century 'Poor Soul's Light'.

Oakridge

A small village, curiously nicknamed locally as 'Little Siberia' or 'Little Russia', with a Victorian church that was built following the efforts of the 19th-century reformer John Keble.

Daneway

A tiny hamlet that lies at the northwestern end of a famous tunnel on the redundant Thames and Severn Canal. Daneway House dates from the 14th century, and was used by Ernest Gimson and the Barnsley brothers, all members of William Morris' Arts and Crafts Movement.

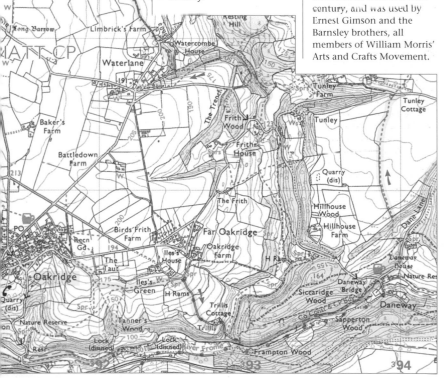

The sturdy Town Hall lies at the heart of Tetbury

ST SAVIOUR'S CHURCH

St Saviour's Church at Tetbury is on Newchurch Street. Later than St Mary's, it was built, apparently, to accommodate those parishioners whose poverty prevented them from buying a pew in the parish church as the wealthy merchants did.

WOOLSACK RACES

Gumstool Hill in Tetbury is the site of the annual Woolsack Races on Spring Bank Holiday Monday, when teams race each other as they carry a 65-lb bale of wool from the market square and back again.

TETBURY Gloucestershire Map ref ST8993

This is a small, tranquil market town of some charm, set among the broader slopes of the southern Cotswolds, on a promontory overlooking a tributary of the River Avon.

By the 18th century Tetbury was one of the most important cloth market towns of south Gloucestershire. Its main streets radiate from the still impressive market square, dominated by the 17th-century Town Hall or Market House, resting on three rows of tubby Etruscan pillars, but reduced by one storey in 1817. The square is also noted for the Snooty Fox Hotel, the former White Hart. It was rebuilt by the designer of Westonbirt House with entertainment for the Beaufort Hunt in mind.

The road next to the Snooty Fox leads to the Chipping, the site of the old livestock market surrounded by some handsome 18th- and 19th-century houses and the Old Priory. The road continues down to the foot of Gumstool Hill, the scene for the annual Woolsack Races on Spring Bank Holiday Monday.

South from the square, along Church Street, is St Mary's Church, built in Gothic style in the late 18th century. The spire is 186 feet (57m) tall. The interior, lit by Perpendicular-style windows, is coolly elegant. Rows of box pews, with their own entries from the ambulatories, are presided over by panelled galleries and two splendid chandeliers. The ensuing result is magnificent.

Tetbury is home to an unusual museum, at the western end of Long Street, which runs west out of Market Square. The Police Bygones Museum is in the cells of the Old Court House and displays police memorabilia – uniforms and so on – on loan from Gloucestershire Constabulary.

Just over a mile (1.6km) to the north-west of Tetbury is Chavenage, a delightful manor house where Cromwell stayed during his attempt to persuade the owner to accede to the execution of Charles I. There is a fine collection of 17th-century tapestries. The chapel, with a Saxon font found in an estate barn, is close by.

Three miles (4.8km) to the south-west of Tetbury is magnificent Westonbirt Arboretum, where over 13,000 trees thrive in 600 acres of glade and 17 miles (27.2km) of footpaths. The Arboretum was started in 1829 by Sir Robert Holford of Westonbirt House. This is a 19th-century neo-Elizabethan building designed by Lewis Vulliamy who was responsible for the Snooty Fox in Tetbury and the Dorchester Hotel in London.

ULEY AND OWLPEN Gloucestershire Map ref ST7898
Uley, a large, pretty village of 18th-century houses that scuttle down the hillside into a deep valley, became prosperous through the wool dyeing industry, famous for its 'Uley Blue'. There is still a functioning brewery, whilst the Crown is a fine pub.

Uley Bury overlooks the town – it is a classic site for a hillfort, a small flat 32-acre plateau surrounded by particularly steep slopes. It was occupied by the Dobunni, the native tribe overrun by the Romans, but there are indications of occupation during the Neolithic period. A short walk is recommended for its spectacular views – see Walk on page 96.

North of Uley, towards Frocester Hill, is Hetty Pegler's Tump, a 180-foot (55m) Neolithic barrow, surrounded by a stone wall and with a long central chamber which can be entered, uncomfortably, by obtaining the key from a nearby cottage.

East of Uley, within striking distance by foot, is Owlpen Manor, a beautifully sited 15th-century manor house restored by Norman Jewson in the 1920s. Close by is the 19th-century church and 18th-century mill.

WESTONBIRT ARBORETUM
Managed by the Forestry Commission, Westonbirt Arboretum contains one of the most important collections of trees and shrubs in the world and is beautiful at any time of year – marvellous displays of flowers in spring, shady glades in summer, the mellow russets and yellows of autumn and the Siberian grandeur of winter. There is a visitor centre with an exhibition, shop and interesting video programme.

Pretty gardens with high yew hedges frame Owlpen Manor

Discover Uley Bury

This short and easy walk offers some marvellous views across the Severn Estuary to the hills and mountains beyond. One fairly steep climb, otherwise good woodland paths and grassy tracks.

Time: 1½ hours. Distance: 2½ miles (4km).
Location: 7 miles (11.3km) southwest of Stroud.
Start: Uley village on the B4066 between Stroud and Dursley.
Park near the post office on the main street.
(OS grid ref: ST790984.)
OS Map: Explorer 168 (Stroud, Tetbury & Malmesbury)
1:25,000 .
See Key to Walks on page 121.

ROUTE DIRECTIONS

Take the narrow lane to the right of **Uley** post office, pass between some houses as it becomes a track, then before reaching a stile in front of you, turn right on to an enclosed path in the direction of the church. Pass beside wooden fencing, with glimpses of the church ahead of you to the right, and when

the churchyard can be seen on the right, turn left along a narrow unmarked path beside a cottage. Ascend more steeply between hedges, passing a cottage on the left, to a kissing gate and a steeply rising meadow, noting the lovely views that open up behind you across the roofs of Uley to **Owlpen Manor**.

At the tree line stay left of the woods and, in the corner on the right, pass through a bridle gate to join a meandering woodland path that climbs above a wider path to your left. On reaching a wire fence, keep to the path as it bears left, then shortly climb a stile and continue your ascent to the woodland fringe. Continue on the path as it climbs across grassland to a junction. Turn right to follow the contours of the hill in an anti-clockwise direction, with a steep drop to the right. Eventually come to another junction of paths and tracks. Turn left on to a track which runs along the edge of the hill, **Uley Bury**, with splendid views across the River Severn and the Forest of Dean. At the next corner, disregard the waymarked stile to your right, and continue round the hill with views across the village of Dursley to the cenotaph-like William Tyndale monument which can be seen in the distance.

On reaching the southwest corner of Uley Bury, bear right on a path between hummocks and begin to descend steeply through the undergrowth, keeping left. Follow this path steeply downhill to a stile. Cross into a meadow and then on to a tarmac path. Follow this path all the way to a cottage at the bottom until you come

Wet your whistle with a drop of Uley's own 'Old Spot' ale

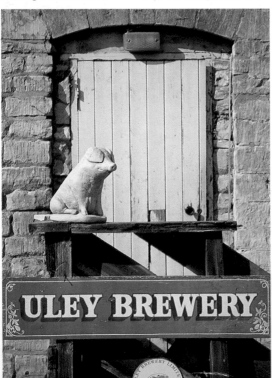

ULEY BREWERY

development as a cloth village before the Industrial Revolution. It was noted, in particular, for the production of blue cloth, Uley Blue. During the Napoleonic wars the population rose dramatically as demand for cloth for the army soared. In 1827 a local man, Edward Sheppard, was one of the first to import Merino wool from Australia.

Owlpen Manor

A fine 15th-century house, with charming gardens, in a delightful setting. Near by is a Victorian church, a medieval tithe barn and a pretty 18th-century mill.

Uley Bury

Uley Bury was once an animal stockade as well as an Iron-Age promontory fort. It is one of the finest examples in the country, covering 30 acres and may have sheltered up to 2,000 people. There are fine views, in all directions, from this vantage point.

to a metal kissing gate in front of you. Go through the gate, walk in front of the cottage, then at a narrow lane, turn left and soon pass the Uley

Looking across to the attractive settlement around Owlpen Manor, in its leafy setting

'Old Spot' brewery to reach the B4066. Turn left along the pavement back into the village centre.

POINTS OF INTEREST

Uley

Uley owes much of its former importance and subsequent prosperity to its

MEMORIAL BRASSES

One of the most beautiful of all Cotswold memorial brasses is to be found in Wotton's church. It lies on the chest tomb of Thomas Berkeley, lord of the manor, who died in 1417, and his wife, Margaret, who predeceased him. The figures are life-size and if you look closely you will see that Lord Berkeley's collar is decorated with little mermaid figures, a reminder of his title of Admiral of the Fleet. Lady Berkeley's head-dress is remarkably beautiful and at her foot is a small dog with a collar, a favourite way of showing us that its mistress was a woman of substance.

Ramsons, or wild garlic, flower beneath the trees on Breakheart Hill, near Wotton-under-Edge

WOTTON-UNDER-EDGE Gloucestershire
Map ref ST7593

Wotton-under-Edge, one of the most interesting small towns in the Cotswolds, is situated just beneath the lip of the Cotswold escarpment. It has a curiously symmetrical street plan and the main road could easily take you through the town without revealing any of its best aspects.

In the Middle Ages Wotton was an important wool town entitled to hold markets and fairs and the Chipping, part of which is now a car park, was the site for them. From the Chipping, Market Street leads past the Star Inn and the Town Hall, to a junction with High Street and Long Street.

On the corner of Market Street and High Street is the red brick Tolsey, granted to the town in 1595 by the Countess of Warwick to serve as the market court. Overlooking the High Street from the other side of Haw Street is the old police station where you can discern the lettering that tells you as much.

Long Street, the main shopping thoroughfare lined with an array of architectural styles, has a lot of character. A diversion along Orchard Street on the right will bring you to the home of Isaac Pitman, inventor of shorthand. At the end of Long Street turn left into Church Street, opposite the 17th-century Falcon Hotel. On the right is a row of delightful almshouses, built in 1638. You may go into the courtyard and visit the little chapel, lit by a pair of depictive stained glass windows.

Church Street crosses Old Town to Culverhay, bringing you to the 18th-century Church Hall, former home to the Blue Coat Church of England School, and the entrance to the parish church, consecrated in 1283, though most of the current building is 15th century. Beyond the churchyard is Potters Pond where the Ram Inn, dating from 1350, is thought to be the oldest building in Wotton.

The Southern Cotswolds

Leisure Information
Places of Interest
Shopping
The Performing Arts
Sports, Activities and the
Outdoors
Annual Events and Customs

Leisure Information

TOURIST INFORMATION CENTRES

Bath
Abbey Chambers, Abbey Churchyard. Tel: 01225 477101.
www.visitbath.co.uk
Cirencester
Corn Hall, Market Place.
Tel: 01285 654180.
Northleach
Cotswold Heritage Centre. Tel: 01451 860715 (seasonal).
Painswick
The Library, Stroud Road.
Tel: 01452 813552.
Stroud
Subscription Rooms, George Street. Tel: 01453 760960.
Tetbury
33 Church Street. Tel: 01666 503552 (restricted winter service).

OTHER INFORMATION

English Heritage
29 Queen Square, Bristol.
Tel: 0117 975 0700
www.english-heritage.org.uk
National Trust
Severn Region, Mythe End House, Tewkesbury. Tel: 01684 850051.
www.nationaltrust.org.uk

Parking
Take care when parking in villages. Do not block drives or entrances to fields.
Bath: A park-and-ride system operates from Newbridge Road; Lansdown; Bath University, Claverton Down. Free parking with buses every 15 minutes to the city centre.

ORDNANCE SURVEY MAPS

Explorer 1:25,000 Sheets 155, 167, 168, 169, 179.
Landranger 1: 50,000 Sheets 162, 163, 172, 173.

Places of Interest

There will be an admission charge at the following places of interest unless otherwise stated.
American Museum
Claverton Manor, Bath.
Tel: 01225 460503. Open late Mar–early Nov, most days.
Arlington Mill Museum
Bibury. Tel: 01285 740368.
Open Easter–Christmas, daily.
Barnsley House Garden
Barnsley. Tel: 01285 740281.
Open all year, certain days.
Bath Abbey Heritage Vaults
Tel: 01225 422462. Open all year, most days.

Bath Book Museum
Manvers Street. Tel: 01225 466000. History and art of bookbinding. Rare books. Open all year, most days. Free.
Bath Postal Museum
8 Broad Street. Tel: 01225 460333. The first postage stamp, the Penny Black, posted here. Open all year, daily.
Beckford's Tower and Museum
Lansdown, Bath. Tel: 01225 460705. Open Apr–Oct, certain afternoons.
British Folk Art Collection
The Countess of Huntingdon's Chapel, The Vineyard, The Paragon, Bath. Tel: 01225 446020. Open all year, most days.
Building of Bath Museum
The Countess of Huntingdon's Chapel, The Vineyard, The Paragon, Bath. Tel: 01225 333895. Open Mar to mid-Dec, most days.
Buscot Park
Buscot. Tel: 01367 242094. 18th-century house in an attractive park. Open Apr–Sep, certain afternoons/weekends.
Chavenage
Tetbury. Tel: 01666 502329. Limited opening.

Chedworth Roman Villa
Near Yanworth. Tel: 01242
890256. Open Mar–Nov, most
days.

Corinium Museum
Park Street, Cirencester. Tel:
01285 655611. Open Apr–Oct,
daily, Nov–Mar, most days.

**Cotswold Countryside
Collection**
Fosseway, Northleach. Tel:
01451 860715. Open Apr–Oct,
daily.

Dyrham Park
Dyrham. Tel: 0117 9372501.
Open: house and garden
Apr–Oct, most afternoons; park:
all year, daily, afternoons.

Frocester Tithe Barn
Frocester Court, Stonehouse.
Tel: 0145382 3250. Open
reasonable daylight hours. Free.

Georgian Garden
Gravel Walk, Royal Victoria Park,
off Queen Square, Bath. Tel:
01225 477760. Open May–Oct,
most days. Free.

Guildhall
High Street, Bath. Tel: 01225
477793. Open all year, most
days. Free.

Heritage Centre
The Chipping, Wotton-under-
Edge. Tel: 01453 521541. Open
all year, most days.

Herschel House and Museum
19 New King Street, Bath.
Tel: 01225 311342. Home of the
18th-century astronome. Open
Mar–Oct, daily; Nov–Feb,
limited opening.

Hetty Pegler's Tump
(Uley Tumulus) Just over 3 miles
(4.8km) northeast of Dursley.
Open all reasonable times.

History of Jeans Museum
Scallywag, York Street, Bath.
Tel: 01225 445040. Open all
year, most days. Free.

**Holburne Museum and
Crafts Study Centre**
Great Pulteney Street, Bath.
Tel: 01225 466669. Open Mar
to mid-Dec, most days.

**Keith Harding's World of
Mechanical Music**
Oak House, High Street,
Northleach. Tel: 01451 860181.
Open all year, daily.

Medieval Hall
High Street, Stroud. Open all
year, daily.

Museum of Bath at Work
Bath Heritage Centre, Julian
Road, Bath. Tel: 01225 318348.
Open Easter–Oct, daily.

Museum of Costume
Assembly Rooms, Bennett Street,
Bath. Tel: 01225 461111. Open
all year, most days.

Museum of East Asian Art
Circus Lodge, 12 Bennett Street,
Bath. Tel: 01225 464640. Open
all year, daily.

Number 1, Royal Crescent
Bath. Tel: 01225 428126. Open
early Mar to mid-Dec, most
days.

Owlpen Manor
Uley. Tel: 01453 860261. Open
Apr–Oct, certain afternoons.

Painswick Rococo Garden
The Stables, Painswick House.
Tel: 01452 813204. Open mid-
Jan to Nov, most days.

Prinknash Abbey Pottery
near Cranham. Tel: 01452
812066. Open all year, daily.

Prinknash Bird Park
near Cranham. Tel: 01452
812727. Open all year, daily.

Priston Mill
Priston Mill, near Bath. Tel:
01225 423894. Open: some
school holidays; Easter–Sep,
limited opening.

Roman Baths Museum
Abbey Square and Stall Street,
Bath. Tel: 01225 477785. Open
all year, daily; evenings in Aug.

Royal Photographic Society
The Octagon, Milsom Street,
Bath. Tel: 01225 462841.
History of photography,
exhibitions. Open all year, daily.

Ruskin Mill
Mill Bottom, Old Bristol Road,
Nailsworth. Tel: 01453 832571.
Arts and crafts centre. Open all
year, daily. Free.

Sally Lunn's
4 North Parade Passage, Bath.
Tel: 01225 461634. Open all
year, daily.

Stroud District Museum
Stratford Park. Tel: 01453
763394. Seasonal opening.

Tetbury Heritage Centre
63 Long Street. Tel: 01666
503552. Open all year, most
days. Free.

**Tetbury Police Bygones
Museum**
The Old Courthouse, 63 Long

Street. Tel: 01666 503552.
Open all year, most days.

Victoria Art Gallery
Bridge Street, Bath. Tel: 01225
477233. Open all year, most
days.

Westonbirt Arboretum
Tel: 01666 880220. Open all
year, daily.

**SPECIAL INTEREST FOR
CHILDREN**

The following places may be of
interest to visitors with children.
Unless otherwise stated, there
will be an admission charge.

Countryside Centre
Bath Road, Haresfield. Tel:
01452 728338. Owls and birds
of prey; walk through aviary.
Open all year, most days.

Norwood Farm
Bath Road, Norton St Philip.
Tel: 01373 834356. Open end
Mar–Sep, daily.

Prinknash Bird Park
near Cranham. Tel: 01452
812727. Open all year, daily.

Rode Bird Gardens
Rode, near Bath. Tel: 01373
830326. Open all year, daily.

Shopping

Bath
Farmers' Market first and
second Sats, Green Park Station.
Market at Twerton on Thu and
Old Down on Sat.
Main shopping areas near the
Abbey; Kingsmead – Union
Street, Stall Street and
Southgate. Exclusive shops in
New Bond Street, Broad Street.
Specialist shops near Upper
Town and off Brock Street.

Cirencester
Farmers' Market second Sat, at
the cattle market.
Street market, Mon and Fri;
cattle market, Tue; antiques
market, Fri.
The main shopping area leads
off the Market Square.

Dursley
Market, Fri.

Fairford
Market, Wed.

Stroud
Farmers' Market first and third
Sat, Corn Hill Market.
Market, Wed, Fri and Sat.

Tetbury
Market, Wed.

LOCAL SPECIALITIES

Crafts
Brewery Arts Centre, Cricklade Street, Cirencester. Tel: 01285 657181. Craft studios: textiles, jewellery, ceramics.
Rooksmoor Mills, Bath Road, Stroud. Tel: 01453 872577. Crafts, gifts, cane furniture.
Pottery
Prinkash Abbey, near Cranham. Tel: 01452 812727
Trout
Bibury Trout Farm, Bibury. Tel: 01285 740215. Other trout farms in the area.

The Performing Arts

Bingham Hall
King Street, Cirencester. Tel: 01285 653313.
Brewery Arts
Brewery Court, Cirencester. Tel: 01285 657181.
Cotswold Playhouse
Parliament Street, Stroud. Tel: 01453 756379.
Prema Arts Centre
South Street, Uley. Tel: 01453 860703.
Theatre Royal
Sawclose, Bath. Tel: 01225 448844.

Sports, Activities and the Outdoors

ANGLING

Fly
Bibury Trout Farm, Bibury. Tel: 01285 740215. Lechlade Trout Fishery, Burford Road, Lechlade. Tel: 01367 253266.

BALLOONING

Bath
Bath Balloons, 24 Gay Street. Tel: 01225 466888. Heritage Balloons, Kingston House, Pierrepoint Street, Bath. Tel: 01225 318747

BOAT HIRE

Bath
Bath Boating Station, Forester Road. Tel: 01225 466407. Open Apr–Sep.

Equal Venue. Tel: 01225 331647. The John Rennie (private charter only). Tel: 01225 447276.

BOAT TRIPS

Bath
Bath Boating Station, Forester Road. Tel: 01225 466407.

COUNTRY PARKS

Avon Valley Country Park, Keynsham. Tel: 0117 9864929. Open Apr–Oct, most days.

CYCLE HIRE

Bath
Avon Valley Cyclery, Arch 37, rear of Bath Spa Station. Tel: 01225 461880.
Cyclists Touring Club. Tel: 01225 834095.

GLIDING

Aston Down
Cotswold Gliding Club, Aston Down Airfield. Tel: 01285 760415.
Nympsfield
Bristol & Gloucestershire Gliding Club. Tel: 01453 860342.

GOLF COURSES

Dursley
Stinchcombe Hill Golf Club. Tel: 01453 542015.
Minchinhampton
Minchinhampton Golf Club, New Course. Tel:01453 833866. Old Course. Tel: 01453 832642.
Painswick
Painswick Golf Club, Golf Club Lane. Tel: 01452 812180.
Wotton-under-Edge
Cotswold Edge Golf Club, Upper Rushmire. Tel: 01453 844167.

HORSE RACING

Bath
Bath Racecourse, Lansdown. Tel: 01225 424609.

HORSE-RIDING

Minchinhampton
Hyde Riding Centre. Tel: 01453 882413.
Stroud
Camp Riding Centre, The Camp. Tel: 01285 821219.
Wellow
Wellow Trekking Centre. Tel: 01225 834376.

LANDROVER SAFARIS

Cotswold Edge Landrover, Hillersley, Star Hill, Nailsworth. Tel: 01453 833816.

POLO

Cirencester
Polo matches at Cirencester Park each Sun May–Sep. Entry via A419 Stroud Road.

WATERSPORTS

South Cerney
Cotswold Water Park. Keynes Country Park, Shorncote, Cirencester. Tel: 01285 861459.

Annual Events and Customs

Badminton
Badminton Horse Trials. May.
Bath
Literature Festival. Feb or March; International Festival May/June; Mozartfest in November.
Bisley
Blessing of the Wells, Ascension Day.
Cirencester
Festival of the arts, June.
Fairford
Air Tattoo, July.
Gatcombe
Horse Trials in July or August.
Painswick
Clypping Ceremony, late Sep.
Tetbury
Woolsack Races and Fayre. May.

Automaton at Keith Harding's World of Music

The Oxfordshire Cotswolds

The distinctive character of the Cotswolds does not quite respect county boundaries. Where Gloucestershire ends the villages of honeyed limestone, watered by pretty streams and set amid rolling sheep pastures, continue into Oxfordshire and Warwickshire. With the well-known exceptions of Burford and Woodstock, many of these unspoilt villages, with their medieval wool churches and charming cottages, are frequently and undeservedly overlooked. Whilst many are described in the text on the following pages, a few others, particularly those of Warwickshire, are included in Car Tour 1 on page 20.

Burford's charming main street slopes down the hill to a medieval bridge at the bottom

BURFORD Oxfordshire Map ref SP2512
Just off the main Oxford road, Burford is all but invisible to passing motorists. Drive north from the roundabout, however, and almost immediately, from the brow of the ridge, Burford slips away before you in a sedate cascade of handsome inns and charming cottages. The wide main street, lined with shops and pubs, passes the church to the right before crossing the Windrush on a medieval bridge of 1322, by the old mill.

Burford church has a fascinating history; note the elaborate 'bale tombs' which date back to about 1660

BURFORD BAIT
In the days immediately following the opening of the turnpikes, when Burford was an important coaching town, its inns competed with each other for travellers' custom. 'Burford Bait' was the name given to the famously large meals they provided, probably based on venison poached from Wychwood Forest.

Burford's prosperity over the centuries has depended on three factors – wool, quarrying, and coaching. There were burgesses here in the 13th century and the town grew rapidly to become an important wool centre. The nearby quarries at the Barringtons, Upton and especially Taynton produced some of the most notable stone in the Cotswolds and much of it went to build some of England's finest buildings – Blenheim Palace, St Paul's Cathedral and various Oxford colleges. The Barringtons also produced the Strongs, a family of masons – Sir Thomas Strong was Christopher Wren's master mason in the construction of St Paul's. Another eminent family of masons, the Kempsters, came from Upton and Burford.

A fillip for Burford came with the dawn of the coaching era from the 18th century, when the town was an important stop on the route to Oxford and London. This came to an end with the railway, which happened to bypass Burford.

Burford is a delight to stroll about. Whilst the High Street is the main thoroughfare, Sheep Street to the west, and Witney Street and Church Lane to the east, have much to offer. Along Sheep Street there are some very

ROYAL APPOINTMENT
Another speciality of Burford was the saddlery business. This was in part, at least, a result of the proximity of the Bibury races which used to take place on the course near Aldsworth. Burford saddles received an unspoken royal appointment as a result of the visits of Charles II and his mistress Nell Gwynn who used to stay here when the races were on.

Mellow old almshouses, near the church in Burford

SIMON WISDOM
Opposite the Great Almshouses are the old buildings of Burford Grammar School, founded in 1577 by a wealthy cloth merchant, Simon Wisdom. He was also responsible for the construction of the Weavers' Cottages which are grouped near the medieval bridge.

fine inns – the Bay Tree Hotel and the Lamb Inn (the old brewery next door houses the Tourist Information Centre) – whilst Witney Street boasts perhaps the finest building in the town, the 17th-century Great House, possibly built by the local mason Christopher Kempster. From Witney Street, Guildenford leads to Church Lane where the Great Almshouses, founded in 1457, are close to the church.

The 15th-century parish church is impressive. Among the chapels and monuments, perhaps the finest is the one erected in 1628 to Sir Lawrence Tanfield, Lord Chief Baron of the Exchequer to James I. Another memorial, to Edmund Harman, barber-surgeon to Henry VIII, includes the first representation in Britain of natives of the New World. On the rim of the font the autograph of a Leveller, a Roundhead mutineer kept here for three days during the Civil War, is inscribed: 'Anthony Sedley prisner 1649' (*sic*).

From the High Street, near the bridge, Priory Lane takes you past the handsome Elizabethan Priory, now that rarity, an Anglican convent, to Sheep Street.

Back on the High Street, on the corner of Sheep Street, is the pillared Tolsey, a Tudor house where wool merchants used to meet and which now houses a museum of considerable interest. Further down is the wide arch of the old George Hotel where Charles I used to stay with Nell Gwynn and which later became an important coaching inn.

Three miles (4.8km) to the south of Burford is Cotswold Wildlife Park, set in the grounds of a 19th-century mansion. The varied collection consists of animals from all over the world, with tropical birds, reptiles, an aquarium and insect house.

CHARLBURY Oxfordshire Map ref SP3519
Here is a town which is unexpected in a number of ways.
This area of the Cotswolds hides its villages well in its
folds and on its shelves and Charlbury is a small, busy
town that looks across the Evenlode valley in happy
isolation towards Wychwood Forest. It seems to be self-
sufficient, more or less, with a large number of shops,
inns and a railway station.

Although Charlbury was a sheep town in the past, it
was also famous as a centre of glove manufacture. At the
height of its prosperity, in the mid-19th century, over
1,000 people were employed in the industry.

Behind the main street is a green, the Playing Close,
surrounded by handsome villas and cottages, and solid
iron railings, with a Jacobean-style fountain at one end.
The picture is spoilt, aesthetically speaking, by a dreadful
example of 1960s office architecture across the road.

Charlbury's church, on the other side of the main
street, is largely Perpendicular in style, with a rather
Victorian interior. The town museum is dedicated to the
traditional crafts and industries of the area.

Beyond the River Evenlode is Cornbury Park, a gift
from Elizabeth I to Robert Dudley. A pleasant walk can
be had through the grounds of this largely 17th-century
house, which will also take you across the approach
bridge built in 1689. The house is not open to the public.

Ditchley Park, west of Charlbury, is only occasionally
open to the public. The fine 18th-century mansion was
built for the 2nd Earl of Lichfield by James Gibbs, with
landscaping by 'Capability' Brown. The house was a
meeting place for Winston Churchill and President
Roosevelt during World War II.

LITERARY ASSOCIATIONS
Finstock, a couple of miles
south of Charlbury, has
several literary associations.
The great poet T S Eliot was
baptised into the church here
in 1927, whilst the novelist
Barbara Pym, who died in
1980, lived here for the last
eight years of her life.

*The neo-Jacobean drinking
fountain at Charlbury,
scattered with chestnut
blossom*

Church and River Valley

A pleasant walk that explores the most easterly
reaches of the Cotswolds, just inside the Oxfordshire
border. Beginning from Burford, one of the finest small
towns in the Cotswolds, this fairly easy going ramble
incorporates the picturesque Windrush Valley and the
lonely church at Widford, set on the banks of the river.
Some paths may be muddy after wet weather.

Time: 2¾ hours. Distance: 5¾ miles (9.3km).
Location: 21 miles (33.8km) west of Oxford, off the A40.
Start: Free car park off Witney Street, Burford, east of the High
Street (A361) in the town centre.
(OS grid ref: SP254123.)
OS Map: Outdoor Leisure 45 (The Cotswolds)
1:25,000.
See Key to Walks on page 121.

ROUTE DIRECTIONS

From the car park walk to
Witney Street, turn right and
then right again into **Burford**
main street. Pass the church
and cross the medieval bridge
over the **River Windrush**, to
a roundabout. Turn right,
signposted 'Chipping
Norton', and walk along the
pavement through Fulbrook.
Pass the church and the
Mason's Arms.

Turn right through a gap at
the end of a high stone wall
on to a short path to a field.
Bear diagonally left to the far
corner (if in crop it may be
best to follow the right-hand
field edge), turn left around
the field edge, with farm
buildings visible ahead, to a
gap in another hedge or wall
into a smaller field. Head
diagonally right to a gap in
the corner of the field, then
bear slightly left across the
next field to join a track and
enter Widley Copse.

Turn right through the
woodland (can be muddy),
then, as you emerge from the
trees, pass a track on the left
and continue between a wall
and hedge. The track then
bears right and begins to
descend towards houses and
farm buildings.

Pass Paynes Farm Cottages
and go through Paynes Farm,
then shortly, as the surfaced
lane dips sharply left, turn
hard right up a track towards
woodland. Proceed ahead
through a field, keeping the
woodland to your right, then
follow the track downhill into
a dip and go through a gate.
Remain on the track between
hedges to a country lane.
Turn right, and where the
road dips, turn left over a stile
into a grassy valley. Continue
to a stile, keep ahead towards
a house, with Widford church
coming into view to your
right.

At a T-junction of tracks,
just before the house, turn
right and go through a
gateway, then pass **Widford**
church on your right and

proceed to a lane. Turn left,
then shortly cross the River
Windrush, and turn right at a
T-junction of roads. After 200
yards (183m), bear off right
across a stile and walk parallel
with the river, crossing several
stiles and fields, until, when
you can see Burford church
on the right, you rejoin the
road just outside Burford.
Turn right, then very soon
walk along the footway back
along Witney Street to
Burford town centre and the
car park.

POINTS OF INTEREST

Burford

Burford, one of the loveliest
Cotswold towns, was a
Saxon settlement, and an
important place on the
ancient route between
Wessex and Mercia. Lying in
good sheep country, it
became an important cloth
centre by the 16th century
and many of the town's
beautiful buildings are due
to the wealth of the cloth
merchants of the period.
Most striking perhaps, with
its graceful spire, is the

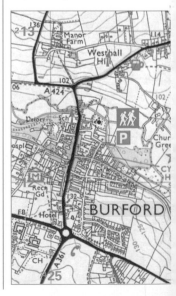

church, which is said to stand on the site of a Roman villa and incorporates mosaics dating from AD 100. Near Burford are some of the quarries that produced the stone for St Paul's Cathedral in London.

River Windrush

Rising in the high wolds above Winchcombe, the River Windrush flows eastwards to become one of the most picturesque of Cotswolds rivers. Its name is derived from the Anglo-Saxon 'wen', or meander and 'risc' or rush.

Widford

Widford church is small and curiously isolated; yet in the late 14th century there were

at least 13 households serving it. By the early 15th century there were only three, the others, presumably, were victims of the Black Death. The church may stand on the site of the burial place of St Oswald

The little church at Widford lies in isolation, its settlement long gone

who died here on his way to Gloucester from Lindisfarne. Within the church are 14th-century murals.

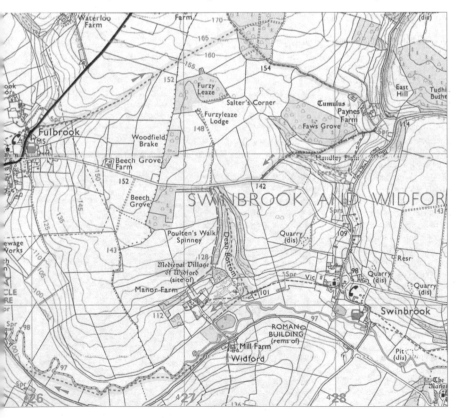

CHURCHILL

Just 3 miles (4.8km) southwest of Chipping Norton is the village of Churchill, the birthplace of Warren Hastings, the first Governor-General of India. It was also the birthplace of William Smith, 'the Father of English Geology', who produced the first geological map of England.

CHIPPING NORTON Oxfordshire Map ref SP3127

This busy market town, the highest in Oxfordshire at 650 feet (197m), is distinguished at its outskirts by the large Victorian tweed mill, now converted to flats, that sits in a fold to the west of the town. The Bliss Tweed Mill, built in 1872 by the Lancashire Architect George Woodhouse, only closed in 1980 and is an unusual reminder, in the Cotswolds, of the Industrial Revolution; and yet there is something disconcertingly memorable about this example of the Victorian age.

The heart of Chipping Norton is the Market Square which is dominated by the 19th-century Town Hall, with its Tuscan-style portico, and a varied collection of shops, hotels and houses dating back to the 17th century, though most are 18th century – a testimony to a former prosperity based on the wool trade.

From the square, the town slopes down Church Street past a row of almshouses dating back to 1640 towards St Mary's, a Perpendicular church containing some fine brasses and impressive tombs. Its most unusual feature is the hexagonal porch with a vaulted ceiling. Behind the church are the motte and bailey earthworks which show that the town was already of some importance in the Norman period.

In Middle Row look for the 16th-century Guildhall. Chipping Norton is one of the few towns in the area blessed with a theatre, which is particularly well known for its pantomimes.

Curtains at the high windows of Bliss Mill reveal its new function as dwelling apartments

FILKINS Oxfordshire Map ref SP2304

A quiet Cotswold village which has a distinctly bypassed feel about it. Its cottages are distinguished for their solid craftsmanship rather than their beauty, and their story can be read in an entertaining book, *Jubilee Boy*, (on sale at the woollen mill, among other places) by an ancient local resident, George Swinford. He worked as a foreman on the estate belonging to the British statesman, Sir Stafford Cripps, and has also given his name to Swinford Museum of Rural Life.

The village is best known, however, for its working woollen weaving factory, one of the last, if not the last, in the Cotswolds, a rather poignant fact when it is considered that the very landscape of the area owes its form to sheep. But Cotswold Woollen Weavers keeps the flag flying, producing quality clothes, on clattering old looms, to suit most tastes. The factory premises are an attractive old barn. All the processes of production can be watched and, whilst it is a serious business concern, the historical relevance of wool production is not overlooked, for there is a permanent exhibition devoted to sheep and wool. There is also a café, an art gallery and an excellent shop. Adjoining buildings contain more workshops devoted to other traditional crafts.

A short distance east of Filkins are some interesting little villages. The south doorway of the church at Kencot dates back to the 12th century and is decorated with a carving of Sagittarius shooting an arrow into the mouth of a monster. The church at Alvescot, in a quiet location to the north of the village, has a splendid 16th-century brass.

Traditional patterns are still woven at the mill in Filkins, a complement to the Museum of Rural Life

QUARRY WORKERS
The last people to work some of the quarries in the Filkins' area, before they were reopened by George Swinford in 1929, were French prisoners of war from the Battle of Waterloo.

The memorial plaque in Kelmscot village celebrates the artist William Morris

MORRIS MEMORIAL HALL
Kelmscot's Morris Memorial Hall, the village hall, was designed by an important member of the Arts and Crafts Movement, Ernest Gimson, and it was opened by the great playwright, George Bernard Shaw in 1933. The site was a gift from Lord Faringdon, whilst the stone came from the nearby quarry at Filkins, owned by Sir Stafford Cripps, and was similarly offered as a gift. Gimson died before its completion and the work was carried out by a local builder, Mr King of Lechlade.

KELMSCOT Oxfordshire Map ref SU2499
A small village, the fame of which is inseparable from the 19th-century poet and artist, William Morris. On the façade of a terrace of cottages on the main street, there he is in carved relief seated in the shade of a tree, knapsack and hat at his side. Kelmscot Manor, on the edge of the village, was his home from 1871 until his death in 1896. He is buried in the local churchyard in a grave modelled on a Viking tomb.

Kelmscot Manor is open to the public according to a limited timetable. Built in the late 16th century, Morris only rented it but it now contains a fine collection of items associated with the man and with his craft, most notably those comparatively simple, domestic, artefacts that he strove to see reinvigorated through the Arts and Crafts Movement (see page 90). That this village came to mean so much to him is clear from the fact that he called his own private printing press, established in London, after it and from the following, unashamedly sentimental lines:

'The wind's on the wold and the night is a-cold
And the Thames runs chill twixt mead and hill
But kind and dear is the old house here
And my heart is warm amidst winter's harm'.

MINSTER LOVELL Oxfordshire Map ref SP3111
Here is a small village of particular interest. It is, first of all, exceptionally pretty – a fine old bridge spans the Windrush and the main street is lined with an even mixture of Cotswold stone and thatch.

At the far end of the street, where it narrows and rises a little, you can park and then walk down to the church. It used to be accompanied by a priory, but it was dissolved in 1414. The remaining church, however, is quite beautiful. Its beauty is less evident from the outside, but once you go in, the perfection of its design becomes obvious. It is welcoming and comforting, well-tended like a cared-for drawing room, yet uplifting and peaceful. Cruciform in shape, it was built in 1431 on the foundations of an earlier 12th-century church. It lacks only the warming colours of stained-glass windows and some of the other humanising features that have gone in the last few hundred years. But the font is original and the alabaster tomb is thought to be of William, 7th Baron Lovell, who built the church.

Behind the church, on the banks of the Windrush, stands the romantic ruin of Minster Lovell Hall built, like the church, by William Lovell. Originally a fortified manor house on a grand scale, it was sold to Sir Edward Coke whose descendants dismantled it in 1747, the remains finding use as farm buildings until the 1930s. A short stroll from the Hall, across the field among other farm buildings and also open to the public, is the sturdy, round, medieval dovecote.

A short distance from Minster Lovell, and a pleasant walk along the river, is the pretty village of Crawley with a river bridge and an old blanket mill.

Just to the south of Minster Lovell lie the Charterville Allotments, the subject of a 19th-century social experiment. The 300 acres were purchased by an early socialist and offered as smallholdings to poor families, along with £30 and a pig. The experiment failed but some of the cottages remain.

A MACABRE LEGEND

Several legends attach themselves to Minster Lovell Hall. The strangest concerns Francis Lovell, a Yorkist, who fled after the Battle of Bosworth, returning in 1487 to champion the cause of the pretender, Lambert Simnel. Defeated at the Battle of Stoke, Lovell returned to the Hall and locked himself in a secret room, attended by a dog and a servant. Somehow, when the servant died, Lovell became trapped in the room and died there. In 1708, during work on the house, a skeleton was apparently discovered seated at a desk, with a dog at its feet.

The splendid ruins of Minster Lovell Hall stand in a loop of the River Windrush

Uneven monoliths in the curve of the King's Men, part of the Rollrights

HOOK NORTON

Hook Norton, east of Great Rollright, is known these days, above all, for its beer. Brewed in a Victorian red-brick brewery, Hook Norton Ale is affectionately known as 'Hooky'. The village's former importance as an ironstone centre is evident from the remains of a huge railway viaduct across the valley.

THE ROLLRIGHT STONES Oxfordshire Map ref SP3031
These ancient monuments, on the side of the A3400 Stow road not far from Long Compton, consist of two stone circles and a monolith.

The three elements of the Rollright Stones have each been given a name, the King's Men, the Whispering Knights and the King Stone, which derive from a legend explaining their origins. Long ago a band of soldiers met a witch who told them that if their leader were to take seven long strides and 'if Long Compton thou canst see, King of England thou shall be'. The aspiring monarch risked all, saw nothing and was, along with his followers, turned to stone. The Whispering Knights are the traitors who planned to overthrow the king once he became ruler of all England.

The facts are more banal. The 70 King's Men, 100 feet (30.8m) in diameter, and the King Stone, which is probably linked with them in some way, are said to date from 2000–1800 BC, during the Bronze Age; their purpose is uncertain. The Whispering Knights are believed to be the remains of a Bronze-Age burial chamber.

The Stones, which can be seen from the A3400, are on private property and are accessible only at the discretion of the owner.

The village of Little Rollright has a fine 17th-century manor house and a handsome little church in the Perpendicular style which contains some magnificent 17th-century monuments.

Great Rollright has fine views southwards over rolling countryside. The only feature of interest is the Norman church with its gargoyles and carved doorway.

Long Compton, strung out along the A3400 not far from the Rollright Stones, is an attractive village with a handsome Perpendicular church approached through a charming lychgate thought to be a cottage with its lower storey removed.

The Rollright Stones are close to the Jurassic Way, a prehistoric route running between the Humber estuary and the southwest of England. That such a route existed suggests a surprising level of contact between peoples throughout the country at an early stage in its history.

SHIPSTON ON STOUR Warwickshire Map ref SP2540
As its name implies, Shipston was for long an important sheep market town. After the demand for local wool began to decline in the 19th century the town continued to flourish thanks to the opening in 1836 of a branch line from the horse-powered tramway built a decade before to link Stratford with Moreton-in-Marsh. The line to Moreton became a modern railway in 1889. Shipston was also an important coaching town, many of the inns from that era surviving in the area of the High Street.

Around Shipston are a number of villages worthy of a look. To the northwest is Ilmington, a lovely scattered village with a fine manor house and a church that contains work by Robert Thompson, the early 20th-century furniture maker and craftsman whose signature was always a wooden mouse. To the north is the attractive village of Honington which is approached by a minor road leading over a five-arched bridge. Just north of Honington is the well-manicured village of Tredington with its fine church and 15th-century spire. To the south of Shipston is Cherington with a selection of pretty 18th- and 19th-century houses.

THE 'MOUSEMAN'
Robert Thompson was a Yorkshire furniture maker whose work can be distinguished by a tiny mouse carved somewhere on the piece. His workshop is still going strong in Kilburn, North Yorkshire, which is well beyond the bounds of this book.

The bridge at Honington, just north of Shipston on Stour

SHIPTON-UNDER-WYCHWOOD Oxfordshire Map ref SP2817

Once the near neighbour of Bruern Abbey, and once the centre of the Wychwood Forest, Shipton is built about a large village green in the Evenlode Valley.

At the lower end of the green is St Mary's Church, begun at the end of the 12th century. It has a fine octagonal spire growing out of its tower, whilst within the church itself there is a 14th-century effigy of a decapitated woman and a Tudor monument of a family group at prayer.

The apparently uniquely named Shaven Crown Hotel, a handsome stone building close to the green, can trace its history back to 1384 and was run at one time by the monks of Bruern Abbey. Bruern was a Cistercian abbey founded in the reign of King Stephen and dissolved in 1539 – nothing now remains. The Shaven Crown, however, once played host to the Fascist leader Oswald Mosley when he was arrested during World War II.

Of Wychwood Forest, one of the last areas of wilderness in Oxfordshire, there is almost nothing left, although it once covered a pretty large area between Stanton Harcourt and Taynton. It was much used by the Normans for hunting and was well known for its deer – indeed the citizens of Burford were entitled to hunt there once each year and the town itself was entitled to two bucks annually. Most English kings up to Charles I, who began to surround the forest with a wall, hunted here. In later centuries many of the notable estate parks in the vicinity – Blenheim and Cornbury, for example – were carved out of it and the only remaining area of forest is a National Nature Reserve which is just 2 miles (3.2km) east of Shipton.

Shipton Court, at Shipton-under-Wychwood, is a typical Cotswold mansion

THE VILLAGES OF THE WINDRUSH VALLEY
Gloucestershire and Oxfordshire

The Windrush rises at Taddington, near Snowshill, and wanders through many villages already mentioned. Beyond Bourton, however, it widens as it approaches the Thames and proceeds through a number of villages to the north of the A40, on the borders of Gloucestershire and Oxfordshire.

Sherborne, on a tributary of the Windrush, has been for centuries part of the Sherborne estate; before that the land was owned by the Abbots of Winchcombe, whose sheep were sheared on the banks of the river every summer. Sherborne House, allegedly haunted by its former owner, John 'Crump' Dutton, the Royalist hunchback, was rebuilt in the 19th century. Occupied by the military during World War II, it then became a boarding school. It now belongs to the National Trust and, although it is not open to the public, there are waymarked walks through the woods and parkland.

The next village to the east is Windrush with a church topped by a fine Perpendicular tower and a magnificent Norman south doorway surrounded by beakheads, bird-like grotesques of mysterious origin. Then come the Barringtons, first Little, then Great, once renowned for their quarries and the local families of masons, the Kempsters and the Strongs, who worked them. No evidence remains of the old subterranean quarries and Little Barrington is a quiet little village, its cottages very prettily clustered about its village green. Near by, the Fox Inn is located by a bridge over the river, built by local master mason Thomas Strong, principal contractor of St Paul's and regarded by Christopher Wren as the leading builder of the day. Great Barrington, to the north, has a Norman church with some fine monuments by the 18th-century sculptor Joseph Nollekens.

The pretty cottages of Little Barrington stretch along the roadside

AN ANCIENT DOOR
A curiosity in Sherborne is a cottage at the eastern end of the village which boasts a complete Norman doorway, removed, presumably, from the earlier church.

WIDFORD CHURCH

The church at Widford takes its name from St Oswald, the Saxon King of Northumbria who was killed in battle in AD 642 by Penda of Mercia. It is conjectured that the church owes its precise location to the fact the saint's body was rested here on its way to burial at Gloucester.

East of Great Barrington lies Taynton, another village that once supplied London and Oxford with its famous prime building stone – taken from open-cast quarries, it was transported overland to Lechlade and thence by barge to London. Beyond it is Burford (see page 102) and then Widford church, the poignant remains of a once thriving village that simply disappeared, probably as a result of the plague. The 13th-century church, small and solitary on a mound overlooking the river, is worth a look for its rows of box pews, and the wall paintings which date from the 14th century .

A short way from Widford is Swinbrook, a village associated with the Mitford family, particularly five of Lord Redesdale's daughters, Nancy, Diana, Unity, Jessica and Deborah. Unity became a close friend of Adolf Hitler, Diana married the British fascist leader, Sir Oswald Moseley, Deborah became the Duchess of Devonshire, whilst Nancy and Jessica became well-known writers. Nancy and Unity are buried in the graveyard of the church, which contains the wonderful triple-decker monument to the Fettiplace family who once owned a mansion here. Across the river to the southeast is Asthall, a charming village with a fine Elizabethan manor.

WITNEY Oxfordshire Map ref SP3510

Another Windrush town, Witney remains famous for its blankets, the production of which somehow managed to survive the collapse of the Cotswold woollen industry after the Industrial Revolution.

The Market Square is the centre of the town and contains an unusual 17th-century Butter Cross and the 18th-century Town Hall. Beyond, near a green, is the

A sundial atop the Butter Cross offers an alternative time in Witney

13th-century church, complete with its massive tower, and a fine collection of houses which date from the 17th and 18th centuries.

In the High Street is the Blanket Hall, built in 1721 by the Company of Blanket Weavers, a group of prosperous weavers who were granted their charter in 1711.

Just to the southeast of Witney, and well-signposted on the A40, is the Cogges Manor Farm Museum, reflecting farming life in the Edwardian period. Among the machinery and livestock, you will find a working kitchen and dairy.

WOODSTOCK Oxfordshire Map ref SP4416

A small town of some charm, most famous as the home of the Churchill family, whose ancestral home is Blenheim Palace. It has always enjoyed royal patronage, however, since Henry I built a park and hunting lodge here in the 12th century, which his grandson, Henry II, preferred to use to entertain his mistress, the fair Rosamund. The lodge became a palace and the town grew around it. The medieval author of *The Canterbury Tales* and *Troilus and Criseyde*, Geoffrey Chaucer, resided here for some years, whilst in later centuries Woodstock was noted for its glovemaking, an industry which continues in a small way at Woodstock Gloves, on Harrison Lane.

Woodstock palace remained a favourite with the royal family until 1704 when the manor was presented to John Churchill, First Duke of Marlborough after his success against the French at the Battle of Blenheim. The medieval buildings were subsequently replaced with the magnificent pile that we see today, and christened Blenheim Palace.

LOCAL INDUSTRY
The woollen industry in Witney probably dates back to the Roman period, whilst blanket weaving may have been introduced by the Bishop of Winchester who had a palace here – certainly weaving is mentioned in the 12th century in the accounts of the local Manor Courts.

PALATIAL PLAYGROUND
The grounds of Blenheim offer other distractions – there is a butterfly house and a children's playground and it is possible to hire rowing boats on Blenheim Lake. The park is also the venue for various events held throughout the year.

Blenheim is one of the great palaces of England, and set in superb grounds

A DEMANDING EMPLOYER
A prodigious display of ill feeling, in keeping with the magnitude of the undertaking, accompanied the construction of Blenheim Palace. The design is the work of Sir John Vanbrugh (who also built Castle Howard in Yorkshire) but in Sarah Jennings, the wife of the Duke of Marlborough, he found himself in the hands of a demanding employer whose caprices finally led him to resign the commission in 1716, fortunately after most of the work had been accomplished. Although Nicholas Hawksmoor oversaw the final construction, it was, however, largely the Duchess' tenacity that ensured completion of the building after the death of her husband – not only did she find the money when Queen Anne's government failed to stump up all the promised funds, she was also responsible for much of the interior design.

Woodstock sports a number of excellent hostelries, including the creeper-clad Bear Hotel

Designed by John Vanbrugh, it is perhaps the greatest palace in England, its Baroque extravagance brilliantly humanised by the beauty of the 2,000-acre park, landscaped by 'Capability' Brown. The beauty of the relationship between the palace and its grounds can best be appreciated by walking from the town and entering the park through Nicholas Hawksmoor's Triumphal Arch, or the Woodstock Gate, just off Park Street. Merely to walk around the palace, cross the Grand Bridge and explore the views as you walk to the Column of Victory, is breathtaking, but you can also enjoy a rose garden and the world's largest symbolic hedge maze.

The palace itself is replete with gilt and grandeur – carvings by Grinling Gibbons, Flemish tapestries illustrating the martial valour of the duke, and a fine collection of paintings. In the Great Hall is the magnificent ceiling painted by Sir James Thornhill, whilst the Long Library is one of the longest single rooms in Britain. The first duke and duchess are buried in the chapel, built by Hawksmoor in 1731. The room where Sir Winston Churchill was born is the focal point of an exhibition devoted to his life.

The town of Woodstock is, itself, worthy of some exploration. The streets that cluster around the 18th-century Town Hall are lined with a fine assortment of houses and inns from the 17th and 18th centuries. The most famous is the Bear Hotel, which dates back to the 13th century. The Parish Church of St Mary Magdalen is set in a charming churchyard and is surmounted by a classical tower of 1785. The Norman south doorway is particularly fine.

Opposite the church is Fletcher's House, built for a 16th-century merchant and which now houses the Oxford County Museum, devoted to the history and traditions of Oxfordshire. The elegant townhouse also has pleasant gardens. The town stocks are preserved at the museum entrance.

The Oxfordshire Cotswolds

Leisure Information
Places of Interest
Shopping
The Performing Arts
Sports, Activities and the
Outdoors
Annual Events and Customs

Checklist

Leisure Information

TOURIST INFORMATION CENTRES

Burford
The Brewery, Sheep Street.
Tel: 01993 823558.
Chipping Norton
The Guildhall, Goddards Lane.
Tel: 01608 644379 (seasonal).
Witney
Town Hall, Market Square.
Tel: 01993 775802.
Woodstock
Oxford County Museum, Park
Street. Tel: 01993 813276
(seasonal).

OTHER INFORMATION

English Heritage
29 Queen Square, Bristol.
Tel: 0117 975 0700.
www.english-heritage.org.uk
National Trust
Severn Region, Mythe End
House, Tewkesbury. Tel: 01684
850051.
www.nationaltrust.org.uk

ORDNANCE SURVEY MAPS

Explorer 1:25,000 Sheet 180.
Landranger 1: 50,000 Sheets
151, 163, 164. Outdoor Leisure
1:25,000 Sheet 45.

Places of Interest

There will be an admission
charge at the following places of
interest unless otherwise stated.
Blenheim Palace
Woodstock. Tel: 01993 811325.
Palace and garden Mar–Oct,
daily; park all year, daily.
**Cogges Manor Farm
Museum**
Church Lane, Witney.
Tel: 01993 772602. Open early
Apr–late Oct, most days.
Cotswold Wildlife Park
Burford. Tel: 01993 823006.
Open all year, daily.
**Minster Lovell Hall and
Dovecot**
Minster Lovell. Tel: 01993
775315. Open all year, daily.
Free.
Oxford County Museum
Fletcher House, Park Street,
Woodstock. Tel: 01993 811456.
Open May–Sep, daily. Free.
**Swinford Museum of Rural
Life**
Filkins. Tel: 01367 860334.
Limited opening.
Tolsey Museum
High Street, Burford. Tel: 01367
810294. Open Mar–Oct.

Shopping

The main shopping areas are
Charlbury, Chipping Norton
(market, Wed), Burford, Witney.
Chipping Norton
Farmers' Market, fourth Friday,
Market Square.
Witney
Farmers' Market, third Thursday,
Church Green.

LOCAL SPECIALITIES

Wool
Cotswold Woollen Weavers,
Filkins. Tel: 01367 860491.
Adjoining craft workshops

The Performing Arts

Chipping Norton Theatre
Spring Street, Chipping Norton.
Tel: 01608 642350.

Sports, Activities and the Outdoors

GOLF COURSES

Burford
Burford Golf Course, Swindon
Road. Tel: 01993 822583.

HORSE-RIDING

Nether Westcote
Far Furlong Stables. Tel: 01993
831193.

Annual Events and Customs

Burford
Gloucestershire Guild of
Craftsmen Spring Exhibition.
May/June.

120

Atlas and Map Symbols

THE NATIONAL GRID SYSTEM

The National Grid system covers Great Britain with an imaginary network of 100 kilometre grid squares. Each square is given a unique alphabetic reference as shown in the diagram. These squares are sub-divided into one hundred 10 kilometre squares, each numbered from 0 to 9 in an easterly (left to right) direction and northerly (upwards) direction from the bottom left corner. Each 10 km square is similarly sub-divided into one hundred 1 km squares.

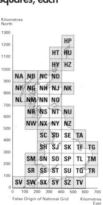

KEY TO ATLAS

⛪	Abbey, cathedral or priory	-----	National trail
🐠	Aquarium	NT	National Trust property
⛫	Castle	NTS	National Trust for Scotland property
⌒	Cave	🦌	Nature reserve
🦌	Country park	★	Other place of interest
🏏	County cricket ground	P·R	Park and Ride location
🐄	Farm or animal centre	⚘	Picnic site
··········	Forest drive	🚂	Steam centre
✿	Garden	🎿	Ski slope natural
⛳	Golf course	🎿	Ski slope artifical
🏠	Historic house	ℤ	Tourist Information Centre
🐎	Horse racing	☀	Viewpoint
🏁	Motor racing	V	Visitor or heritage centre
🏛	Museum	🦁	Zoological or wildlife collection
📞	AA telephone		Forest Park
✈	Airport		Heritage coast
Ⓗ	Heliport		National Park (England & Wales)
🌾	Windmill		National Scenic Area (Scotland)

KEY TO ATLAS

MOTORWAY		A ROAD	
M4	Motorway with number	A1123	Other A road single/dual carriageway
Fleet	Motorway service area	======	Road tunnel
Toll	Motorway junction with and without number	Toll	Toll
	Restricted motorway junctions		Road under construction
	Motorway and junction under construction		Roundabout
PRIMARY ROUTE		B ROAD	
A3	Primary route single/dual carriageway	B2070	B road single/dual carriageway
Grantham North	Primary route service area		B road interchange junction
BATH	Primary route destinations		B road roundabout with adjoining unclassified road
	Roundabout		Steep gradient
5	Distance in miles between symbols		Unclassified road single/dual carriageway
	Narrow Primary route with passing places		Railway station and level crossing

KEY TO TOURS

	Tour start point	Buckland Abbey	Highlighted point of interest
➡	Direction of tour		
▪▪–▪▪	Optional detour		Featured tour

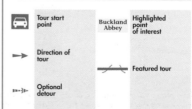

KEY TO WALKS

Scale 1:25,000, 2½ inches to 1 mile, 4cm to 1 km

🥾	Start of walk	Line of walk
➡️	Direction of walk	⊪⊪⊪⊪ Optional detour
	Buckland Abbey	Highlighted point of interest

ROADS AND PATHS

M1 or A6(M)	M1 or A6(M)	Motorway
A 31(T) or A35	A 31(T) or A35	Trunk or main road
B 3074	B 3074	Secondary road
A 35	A 35	Dual carriageway
		Road generally more than 4m wide
		Road generally less than 4m wide
		Other road, drive or track
		Path

Unfenced roads and tracks are shown by pecked lines

RAILWAYS

Multiple track / Single track	Standard gauge	Embankment
		Tunnel
Narrow gauge		Road over; road under
Siding		Level crossing
Cutting		Station

PUBLIC RIGHTS OF WAY

Public rights of way may not be evident on the ground

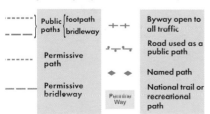

Public paths {footpath / bridleway}	Byway open to all traffic
Permissive path	Road used as a public path
Permissive bridleway	Named path
Pennine Way	National trail or recreational path

The representation on this map of any other road, track or path is no evidence of the existence of a right of way

RELIEF

50 ·	Heights determined by { Ground survey / Air survey }
285 ·	

Contours are at 5 and 10 metres vertical interval

SYMBOLS

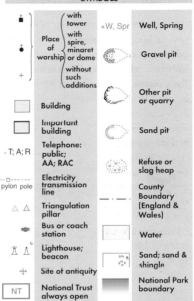

🏛️	Place of worship { with tower	○W, Spr	Well, Spring
●	with spire, minaret or dome		Gravel pit
+	without such additions		
			Other pit or quarry
⬜	Building		
⬜	Important building		Sand pit
· T; A; R	Telephone: public; AA; RAC		
⌐□─── pylon pole	Electricity transmission line		Refuse or slag heap
△ △	Triangulation pillar		County Boundary (England & Wales)
⊯	Bus or coach station		Water
舟 舟	Lighthouse; beacon		Sand; sand & shingle
⊹	Site of antiquity		National Park boundary
NT	National Trust always open		Mud
FC	Forestry Commission		

DANGER AREA

Firing and test ranges in the area
Danger!
Observe warning notices

VEGETATION

Limits of vegetation are defined by positioning of the symbols but may be delineated also by pecks or dots

🌲 🌲	Coniferous trees	○ ○	Non-coniferous trees
△ △	Orchard		Heath
	Coppice		Marsh, reeds, saltings

TOURIST AND LEISURE INFORMATION

⛺	Camp site	PC	Public convenience
ℹ️	Information centre	🅿️	Parking
ℹ️	Information centre (seasonal)	⚡	Viewpoint
🚐	Caravan site	⊕	Mountain rescue post
✕	Picnic site		

Index

Acknowledgements

The author would like to thank the Tourist Information Centres listed in this book for their invaluable assistance.

The Automobile Association wishes to thank the following photographers and libraries for their assistance in the preparation of this book.

MARY EVANS PICTURE LIBRARY 7f
NATURE PHOTOGRAPHERS LTD 6d (P R Sterry)
MANSELL COLLECTION LTD 6f

All the remaining pictures are held in the Association's own library (AA PHOTO LIBRARY) and were taken by S Day with the exception of pages 6g, 7b, 55 which were taken by A Baker; 41b, 58, 92 were taken by P Baker; 7c, 33 were taken by A Lawson; 59, 64, 67 were taken by E Meacher; 6e was taken by K Paterson; 81 taken by R Rainford; 7a, 68 were taken by F Stephenson; 71 taken by R Surman; 3h, 8a, 11a, 26, 27, 30, 31, 45, 46, 47, 72, 73 were taken by W Voysey.